Bleed scripture
pg 81
prayer 155

*Joy unspeakable and full of glory*

IN TODAY'S social-media-saturated world where grammar and friendships are increasingly thin, Michael Haykin's work on Samuel Pearce recalls a time when words and relationships had considerably more heft. Pearce's life and letters reveal a warm spirituality for God, a tender love for his wife and a passionate concern for the lost—all of which serve to break the stereotype of cold-hearted Calvinism so often attributed to British Particular Baptists.

—ANTHONY CHUTE, *Associate Dean and Associate Professor,*
*California Baptist University, Riverside, California*

IN THE SKILLFUL hands of Michael Haykin the life and ministry of Samuel Pearce comes alive for contemporary readers. This well-researched and highly readable book reclaims an often-neglected leader of Calvinist Baptist piety, who stood in close partnership with William Carey and Andrew Fuller. The "seraphic Pearce," as he was often called, invited others to join him in a "holy, happy fellowship with our God." Through Haykin's judicious selections of Pearce's writings that same much-needed invitation is extended today.

—TOM SCHWANDA, *Associate Professor of Christian Formation and Ministry,*
*Wheaton College, Wheaton, Illinois*

THE SHORT LIFE of Samuel Pearce is filled with encouragement, instruction, and inspiration for those who would follow Christ with all their heart. Read the life and letters of Pearce revealed marvelously within these pages and you will also catch the gospel passion that moved Samuel and Sarah Pearce, and their dear friends, William Carey and Andrew Fuller, to launch a movement to take the gospel to the ends of the earth. May readers of this book be inspired likewise to expect great things from God and attempt great things for God.

— GREGORY A. WILLS, *Professor of Church History and Associate Dean,*
*The Southern Baptist Theological Seminary, Louisville, Kentucky*

CALVINISTIC BAPTIST life in England went through a period of extraordinary creativity and growth in the last years of the eighteenth century. This splendid book, the fruit of many years research and reflection, reveals the sort of deep, biblical spirituality which underpinned these advances. Michael Haykin's study of Samuel and Sarah Pearce's piety is superb, and the Pearces' letters, many of which are published here for the first time, are quite simply astonishing. They deserve to take their place alongside those of Samuel Rutherford and be regarded as spiritual classics. If you think this an exaggerated claim then I hope you will read them and end up revising your opinion! I commend this book without reservation, and I hope and pray its influence is both wide and deep.

—**PETER J. MORDEN**, *Tutor in Church History and Spirituality,*
*Spurgeon's College, London, England*

IAIN MURRAY recounts how Jonathan Edwards' *Life of Brainerd* was the one volume, in addition to the Bible, that most shaped the early nineteenth-century missionaries. Similarly, Andrew Fuller noted that Samuel Pearce was like "another Brainerd," and Fuller's *Memoir* of Pearce also proved to inspire those who surrendered worldly comforts for the cause of Christ. How fitting, therefore, for Michael Haykin's new collection of the letters and writings of Samuel and Sarah Pearce to arrive in a day in need of the stirring of the Holy Spirit. This carefully edited and organized volume not only conveys the heart and mind of Pearce but also draws the reader to the glorious work of Pearce's great God. May God bless the reading of this work so that in the coming years, in the darkest corners of the globe, messengers will be found bringing the good news of Christ, led by the Holy Spirit, with the same heart and love for souls as Samuel Pearce.

—**JASON G. DUESING**, *Assistant Professor of Historical Theology,*
*Vice President for Strategic Initiatives, Southwestern Baptist Theological*
*Seminary, Fort Worth, Texas*

L Peace

Classics of Reformed Spirituality

# Joy unspeakable and full of glory

## The piety of Samuel and Sarah Pearce

Edited and introduced by
Michael A.G. Haykin

press

www.joshuapress.com

*Published by*
Joshua Press Inc., Kitchener, Ontario, Canada
*Distributed by*
Sola Scriptura Ministries International
www.sola-scriptura.ca

First published in 2012.

*The publication of this book was made possible by the generous support of:*
*The Ross-Shire Foundation*

Cover and book design by Janice Van Eck

Cover image: Shutterstock
© Cover portrait of Samuel Pearce by Hélène Grondines
Frontispiece portrait of Samuel Pearce from Andrew Fuller, *Memoir of the Late
Rev. Samuel Pearce* (Clipstone: J.W. Morris, 1800)

———

*Library and Archives Canada Cataloguing in Publication is available*

Pearce, Samuel, 1766–1799; Pearce, Sarah Hopkins, 1771–1804
Joy unspeakable and full of glory : the piety of Samuel and Sarah Pearce /
edited and introduced by Michael A.G. Haykin.

(Classics of Reformed spirituality)
Includes bibliographical references

ISBN 978-1-894400-48-0

*To "my invaluable" Alison*
*& to my children, Victoria and Nigel:*
*thank you for everything that*
*makes a book like this possible*

# Contents

# Foreword

Pastoring in Birmingham for the last decade of the eighteenth century, Samuel Pearce faced enormous challenges and opportunities. The century had witnessed a mighty spiritual awakening during which God had raised great preachers, George Whitefield, John Wesley and Daniel Rowland among them. Who would blow the gospel trumpet now with such clarity and unction? The opportunity for missionary expansion was real, and William Carey blazed the trail in India, with an emerging Baptist Missionary Society sharing his vision. In both these respects, Pearce was on the forefront, even though he died aged thirty-three in 1799. It was, however, as the "seraphic Pearce" that he became known among his peers, and as one who mirrored the saintly David Brainerd during his short life, that subsequent generations treasured his legacy. That legacy has been sadly neglected, and the Christian public is indebted to Dr. Haykin and Joshua Press for making it available once more.

Here are some reasons why this book deserves to be read by anyone interested in Reformed piety. Firstly, *it portrays an example of warm personal devotion to the Saviour.* At a critical time in his life while seeking God's will, he spent the day in prayer, fasting and reading Edwards's *Life of Brainerd*. At first his heart was hard as a rock, but then it was as if the Holy Spirit struck the rock with his rod, so that Pearce was refreshed, swallowed up in God, and Christ was all, until, he tells us, "my animal strength was almost exhausted." Such experiences have been the portion of other men of God in similar circumstances: of the Puritan John Flavel and the Welsh Baptist preacher Christmas Evans, to name but two. Pearce was a man in whom a hunger for God was profound, and his dealings with the Saviour were both close and intense. One of his abiding impressions was that "true devotion is found only in those for whom Christ is precious."

Secondly, Pearce had *a passionate burden for the lost*. From the confession of his faith it is clear that he had a strong conviction of the sovereignty and freeness of God's grace in the soul's salvation. His preaching was "with great sweetness and much power," and under his ten-year ministry in Birmingham, he knew of at least 335 brought to faith in Christ. He fully supported William Carey and raised money for his work. Pearce's Calvinism was strong, and for that reason so also was his free and universal offer of the gospel to guilty, miserable, hell-deserving sinners.

Thirdly, he was *a man who humbly submitted to God's will in life and in death*. He was constrained to offer himself for mission work in India, but meekly accepted rejection by those who considered his case. With his health deteriorating at an early age and unable to speak, he prepared for death with dignity and solemnity, resting in God's wise providence and anticipating God's full redemption. Concern for his wife and his congregation reflect selflessness and charity. He urged them to "stand fast in that blessed Gospel which for ten years I have now preached among you."

Reading Dr. Haykin's poignant narrative of Pearce's piety and ministry is a heart-searching exercise, bringing eternity, and God and heaven, closer to the soul's gaze. It is both timely and edifying.
—*Eifion Evans*

# Acknowledgements

In some ways this book has been in the making for twenty-five years. I first read about Samuel Pearce in 1986 and quickly became deeply fascinated by his life and testimony. When Alison—my wife—and I visited the United Kingdom for the first time as a married couple in May of the following year, I made a point of looking at some of Pearce's manuscripts in the archives of the Angus Library, Regent's Park College at the University of Oxford. I saw and read through some of Pearce's letters to his wife Sarah and some of his 68 sermons on the Letter to the Hebrews. I had but a day with those precious texts on that occasion, but it was a day never to be forgotten and gave me a desire to know much more about this remarkable Christian. That day's quick research began a journey that has now lasted two-and-a-half decades, in which I have gone back a good number of times to the Regent's Park College archives to study and transcribe the Pearce manuscripts, and in which I have lectured time and again on Pearce's life and piety, seeking to understand Pearce and his walk with God, and how it can be of value to today's church. I have no hesitation in saying that Pearce's life and ministry represents one of the finest examples of Calvinistic Baptist spirituality in the eighteenth century. Many nineteenth-century readers who read the witness of this Baptist pastor were profoundly changed by their reading. James Waddell Alexander (1804–1859), American Presbyterian pastor and theologian, put it well when he said that "the man who can fail to love when he reads his [i.e. Pearce's] life, can have little sense of the beauty of holiness."[1] For me personally, Pearce's God-centred life has been a deep inspiration, through these years of reading him to live a similar life—to borrow one of his Latin phrases, "*sequor, non aequis passibus*."[2] This book represents part of the fruit of those years of research and reflection.[3]

In editing Pearce's letters, tracts and sermons and his wife's letters, a very few archaic spellings have been modernized, abbreviations have been lengthened, and capitalization, paragraph divisions and punctuation also modernized. Thanks are due a large number of people over these twenty-five years of reading Pearce: Susan J. Mills, the former Archivist of Regent's Park College, for enormous help in working with the Pearce manuscripts; Marina Coldwell, one of the finest secretaries I have ever had, who initially typed a number of these letters; Ruth Engler, who was also involved in typing some of the letters; Dr. Grant Gordon, of Aurora, Ontario, for numerous kindnesses; Dr. Anthony Cross of Regent's Park College, Oxford, England; Dr. Glendon Thompson and the Board of Trustees of Toronto Baptist Seminary and Bible College, for a trip they helped me take in the summer of 2004 to research Pearce; Dr. Ruth E. Mayers Alcalay for research on Pearce and his family in archives in Plymouth and London; Ian Clary, my administrative assistant when I was Principal of Toronto Baptist Seminary and Bible College, and

---

1 Letter to John Hall, August 21, 1825, in John Hall, ed., *Forty Years' Familiar Letters of James W. Alexander* (New York: Charles Scribner, 1870), I, 85.

2 See page 82.

3 The other main part, a critical edition of Andrew Fuller's *Memoirs* of Pearce, will appear hopefully as part of the critical edition of the works of Andrew Fuller.

now again one of my research assistants; Nigel Wheeler, a former doctoral student now pastoring in Lethbridge, Alberta; Scott Bowman, also a former student, now pastoring in the Greater Toronto area; Revd. Emma Walsh, the present librarian of Regent's Park College, the University of Oxford; Ruth Labeth, for her help when she was the librarian at Toronto Baptist Seminary; my maternal aunt, Marie Eyre, for material relating to Birmingham, England; Darrin Brooker for the gift of a copy of Pearce's *Memoirs*; Martha Brown Shepherd, whose husband and children are direct descendants of Samuel and Sarah Pearce through their daughter Anna, for the loan of a book and information regarding the Pearce children; Chisso Wang, currently studying at Toronto Baptist Seminary and Bible College; Linda Durkin, the Faculty Secretary at The Southern Baptist Theological Seminary, who typed the sermons of Pearce; and my daughter, Victoria J. Haykin, who has been a part-time research assistant during the last four summers.

I am also thankful to the staffs of Bristol Baptist College, Bristol, England, the Birmingham City Archives, the American Baptist–Samuel Colgate Historical Library, Rochester, New York, during the 1990s and early 2000s, and to the present and past staff of the Canadian Baptist Archives, McMaster Divinity College, McMaster University, Hamilton, Ontario, for help received on numerous occasions. I am also indebted to Janice Van Eck at Joshua Press for supervising the progress of this book from digital copy to hard copy.

Above all, I am deeply thankful to the God of Samuel Pearce, who providentially brought this choice servant's writings and life across my path. May he, the Triune God, use this little selection of writings from a very different time and world to kindle piety akin to Pearce's in this day and age, and this for his own glory.[4]

---

4 This book was essentially finished in 2008, but its publication was delayed till now. I consider this delay supremely providential, for it was not until June 2011, for example, that I aquired the needed information on Pearce's good friend William Summers and on his beloved wife Sarah.

"Though now ye see him [Christ] not, yet believing, ye rejoice with joy unspeakable and full of glory."—*1 Peter 1:8* (KJV)

---

"A volume of [Pearce's] letters might be collected which would be very valuable."—*John Ryland, Jr.*

---

"I cannot describe to you what pleasure I feel in communion with brethren Pearce, Fuller, and the Northamptonshire ministers in general; I love them, not only because of their views of the gospel, but on account of their being thoroughly given up, in heart and soul to Jesus Christ, and to promote the eternal welfare of their fellow creatures."—*William Ward*

---

"I have read Mr. Fuller's account of Mr. Pearce. It answers the idea I had formed of him, though my personal acquaintance was very slight, but we exchanged a few letters. I believe, if we had lived near together, the paper wall of a denomination would not have prevented our intimacy. He was a man quite to my taste."—*John Newton*

---

"I am reading the *Memoirs of the Rev. Samuel Pearce*, compiled by Andrew Fuller. How the life of such a man shames and condemns that of common Christians. He was pre–eminently a holy man."—*Susan Huntington*

---

"Who can read the lives of a Brainerd, a Whitefield, or a Pearce, without feeling a desire at least to go and do likewise?"—*Joseph Belcher*

# Joy unspeakable
# and full of glory

# The piety of
# Samuel and Sarah Pearce[1]
### 1766-1799 / 1771-1804

The name of Samuel Pearce rarely appears in histories of Christian spirituality, though it most definitely should. His life and thought represent the best of late eighteenth-century Baptist piety. His memoirs, drawn up in 1800 by Andrew Fuller (1754–1815), one

---

1 This study of Pearce's piety draws heavily on no less than ten of the author's earlier studies: "A Singular Submissiveness to the Will of God: Samuel Pearce and Some Extracts from His Diary," *The Evangelical Baptist*, 33, No.8 (June, 1986): 18–19; "Samuel Pearce: Extracts from a Diary: Calvinist Baptist Spirituality in the Eighteenth Century," *The Banner of Truth*, 279 (December 1986): 9–18; "The Spirituality of Samuel Pearce," *Reformation Today*, 151 (May–June 1996): 16–24; "The Spirituality of Samuel Pearce (1766–1799)," *Bulletin of the Canadian Baptist Historical Society*, 2, No.1 (April 1998): 2–10; "Calvinistic Piety Illustrated: A Study of the Piety of Samuel Pearce on the Bicentennial of the Death of his Wife Sarah," *Eusebeia*, 2 (Spring 2004): 5–27; "An "Eminently Christian Spirit": The Missionary Spirituality of Samuel Pearce," *Journal of the Irish Baptist Historical Society*, 11, NS (2004–2005): 25–46; "Introducing Samuel Pearce" in Andrew Fuller, *A Heart for Missions. The Classic Memoir of Samuel Pearce* (Birmingham: Solid Ground Christian Books, 2006), i–vii; "The Spirituality of Samuel Pearce" (http://www.trinity–baptist–church.com/pearce. shtml; accessed March 29, 2008); " "For God's Glory [and] for the Good of Precious Souls": Calvinism and Missions in the Piety of Samuel Pearce," *Puritan Reformed Journal*, 2, No.1 (January 2010): 277–300; "Christian Marriage Illustrated: The Love Letters of Samuel and Sarah Pearce," *The Banner of Truth*, 565 (October 2010): 6–17.

of his closest friends, went through innumerable printings and editions on both sides of the Atlantic in the course of the nineteenth century. Fuller especially focused on Pearce's piety and concluded that the "governing principle in Mr. Pearce, beyond all doubt, was holy love."[2] In fact, for some decades after his death it was not uncommon to hear him referred to as the "seraphic Pearce."[3]

One Baptist friend said of Pearce that "his ardour…gave him a kind of ubiquity; as a man and a preacher, he was known, he was felt everywhere."[4] William Jay (1769–1853), who exercised an influential ministry in Bath for the first half of the nineteenth century, has this amazing remark about Pearce's preaching: "When I have endeavoured to form an image of our Lord as a preacher, Pearce has oftener presented himself to my mind than any other I have

---

2  *Memoirs of the Rev. Samuel Pearce. A.M.* (3rd ed.; Dunstable: J.W. Morris, 1808), 186. Throughout this book this third edition of the memoir has been used, since it represents the final edition that Fuller actually saw through the press. A fourth edition appeared in 1816, the year after Fuller died. To what extent Fuller was able to contribute to it is unclear.

For a book review of the third edition with a note about the changes in it from the two previous editions, see "Account of Religious Publications: Memoirs of the Rev. Samuel Pearce, A.M.," *The Baptist Magazine*, 1 (1809): 374–376. This review ended with this recommendation: "We strongly recommend this volume to all our readers, and we think our brethren in the ministry will be wanting to themselves if they do not give it a very attentive perusal" (376).

For a reprint of an edition of this memoir, see Andrew Fuller, *A Heart for Missions. The Classic Memoir of Samuel Pearce* (Birmingham: Solid Ground Christian Books, 2006).

On Fuller himself, see page 26, footnote 86.

3  See, for example, J.P., "Christians United in Christ," *The Baptist Magazine*, 25 (1833): 256: "the seraphic ardour of Pearce"; *The Life and Letters of John Angell James*, ed. R.W. Dale (3rd ed.; London: James Nisbet and Co., 1861), 67; John Angell James, *An Earnest Ministry the Want of the Times* (4th ed.; London: Hamilton, Adams, & Co., 1848), 272. The phrase appears to have originated with Pearce's friend, John Ryland, Jr.: see Ernest A. Payne, "Samuel Pearce" in his *The First Generation: Early Leaders of the Baptist Missionary Society in England and America* (London: Carey Press, 1936), 46.

4  F.A. Cox, *History of the Baptist Missionary Society, from 1792 to 1842* (London: T. Ward & Co. / G.J. Dyer, 1842), I, 54.

been acquainted with." He had, Jay went on, a "mildness and tenderness" in his style of preaching, and a "peculiar unction." When Jay wrote these words it was many years after Pearce's death, but still, he said, he could see his appearance in his mind's eye and feel the impression that he made upon his hearers as he preached. Ever one to appreciate the importance of having spiritual individuals as one's friends, Jay has this comment about the last time that he saw Pearce alive: "What a savour does communion with such a man leave upon the spirit."[5]

David Bogue (1750–1825) and James Bennett (1774–1862), in their history of the Dissenting interest in England up to the early nineteenth century, have similar remarks about Pearce. When he preached, they said, "the most careless were attentive, the most prejudiced became favourable, and the coldest felt that, in spite of themselves, they began to kindle." But it was when he prayed in public, they remarked, that Pearce's spiritual ardour was most apparent. Then the "most devout were so elevated beyond their former heights, that they said, 'We scarcely ever seemed to pray before.'"[6]

## *"Life in a dear dying Redeemer"*

Pearce was born in Plymouth on July 20, 1766, to William (d. 1805) and Lydia Pearce (d. 1766/1767), devout Baptists.[7] His mother died when he was but an infant, so he was raised by his father, a deacon in the Baptist church at Plymouth, and equally godly grandparents. Initially, after the death of his mother, he went to live with his paternal grandparents at Tamerton Foliot, a village that lay five

---

5  *The Autobiography of William Jay*, eds. George Redford and John Angell James (1854 ed.; repr. Edinburgh: The Banner of Truth Trust, 1974), 372, 373.

6  *The History of Dissenters* (2nd ed.; London: Frederick Westley and A.H. Davis, 1833), II, 653.

7  "Memoir of the Late Rev. Samuel Pearce, A.M.," *The Evangelical Magazine*, 8 (1800): 177.

miles or so north of Plymouth. When he was between eight and ten years old he came back to Plymouth and to his father's care and began to attend the town's grammar school.

As he came into his teen years, he would also have known the nurturing influence of the "sturdy Baptist community" of Plymouth, whose history reached back well into the seventeenth century.[8] The heritage of these Baptists is displayed in the character of one of their early ministers, Abraham Cheare (d.1668).[9] During the great persecution from 1660 to 1688 of all those Christian bodies outside of the Church of England, Cheare was arrested, cruelly treated and imprisoned on Drake's Island, a small island in Plymouth Sound. Fearful that some of his flock might compromise their Baptist convictions to avoid persecution, he wrote a number of letters to his church during the course of his imprisonment. In one of them he cites with approval a statement from the Irenicum (1646) of "holy Burroughs," that is, the Puritan author Jeremiah Burroughs (c.1599–1646). "I desire to be a faithful Minister of Christ and his Church, if I cannot be a Prudent one," Cheare quoted from Burroughs, "standing in the gap is more dangerous and troubelsom [sic] than getting behind the hedge, there you may be more secure and under the wind; but it's best to be there where God looks for a man."[10] Cheare himself was one who "stood in the gap," for he died in 1668 while a prisoner for his Baptist convictions.

As Pearce came into his teen years, however, he consciously spurned the rich heritage of his godly home and the Plymouth Baptist community. According to his own testimony, "several

---

8  Payne, "Samuel Pearce," 47.

9  On Cheare, see John Rippon, "Sketch of the History of Dissenting Churches: History of the Baptist Church at Plymouth" in his ed., *The Baptist Annual Register* (London, 1798–1801), 3:273–282; Joseph Ivimey, *A History of the English Baptists* (London, 1814), II, 103–116; Jeff Robinson, "'A Poor and Despised People':Abraham Cheare and the Calvinistic Baptists at Plymouth" (Unpublished paper given at The Andrew Fuller Center for Baptist Studies annual conference, August 25–26, 2008).

10 *Words in Season* (London: Nathan Brookes, 1668), 250.

vicious school–fellows" became his closest friends, and he set his heart on what he would later describe as "evil" and "wicked inclinations."[11] But God had better plans for his life. In the summer of 1782, a young preacher by the name of Isaiah Birt (1758–1837) came to preach for a few Sundays in the Plymouth meeting-house.[12] The Spirit of God drove home Birt's words to Pearce's heart. The change in Pearce from what he later called "a state of death in trespasses and sins" to a "life in a dear dying Redeemer" was sudden but genuine and lasting.[13] Following his conversion, Pearce was especially conscious of the Spirit's witness within his heart that he was a child of God and of being "filled with peace and joy unspeakable."[14] A year or so later, on the day when he celebrated his seventeenth birthday, he was baptized as a believer and joined the Plymouth congregation in which he had been raised.

Not long after his baptism, the Plymouth congregation perceived that Pearce had been endowed with definite gifts that marked him out as one called to pastoral ministry. So, in November 1785, when he was only nineteen years of age and serving as an apprentice to his father who was a silversmith, Pearce received a call from the church to engage in the ministry of the Word. The church recommended that Pearce first pursue a course of study at the Bristol Baptist Academy. From August 1786 to May 1789, Pearce studied at this school, which was then the sole Baptist institution in Great Britain for the training of ministers for the Calvinistic Baptist denomination. The benefits afforded by this period of study were ones for which Pearce was ever grateful. There was, for example, the privilege of studying under Caleb Evans (1737–1791), the Principal of the Academy, and Robert Hall, Jr. (1764–1831)—the

---

11 Fuller, *Memoirs of the Rev. Samuel Pearce*, 9–10.

12 On Isaiah Birt, see pages 49–53.

13 Samuel Pearce, Letter to Isaiah Birt, October 27, 1782 ("Original Letter from Mr. Pearce to Mr. Birt," *The Evangelical Magazine*, 15 [1807]: 111).

14 Fuller, *Memoirs of the Rev. Samuel Pearce*, 11.

THE PIETY OF SAMUEL AND SARAH PEARCE

former a key figure in the late eighteenth–century Calvinistic Baptist community and the latter a reputed genius and one who was destined to become one of the most celebrated English preachers of the early decades of the next century.[15] Pearce's love for Evans is evident in the funeral sermon he preached when Evans died in 1791.[16]

Then there were the opportunities for the students to preach and try their wings, as it were. A number of years later Pearce recalled an occasion when he went to preach for two consecutive Sundays among the colliers[17] of Coleford, Gloucestershire, the town in which his father in the faith, Isaiah Birt, had grown up. In the week between Pearce "felt particular sweetness" in visiting a number of the colliers in their homes and conversing with them about the things of God and preaching. On one of the evenings, standing on a stone in a hut with a three-legged stool for a podium, he directed thirty or forty of these miners to "the Lamb of God which taketh away the sin of the world." Such an unction attended his preaching that day that the entirety of his hearers were "melted into tears" and he too, "weeping among them, could scarcely speak nor they hear,

---

15 On the life and ministry of Evans, see especially Norman S. Moon, "Caleb Evans, Founder of the Bristol Education Society," *The Baptist Quarterly*, 24 (1971–1972): 175–190; Kirk Wellum, "Caleb Evans (1737–1791)" in Michael A.G. Haykin, ed., *British Particular Baptists, 1638–1910* (Springfield, Missouri: Particular Baptist Press, 1998), I, 213–233; Roger Hayden, *Continuity and Change: Evangelical Calvinism among Eighteenth–Century Baptist Ministers Trained at the Bristol Baptist Academy, 1690–1791* (Milton under Wychwood, Chipping Norton, Oxfordshire: Nigel Lynn Publishing, 2006), 209–240.

On Hall, see, in particular, John Greene, *Reminiscences of the Rev. Robert Hall, A.M.* (2nd ed.; London: Frederick Westley and A.H. Davis, 1834); G.W. Hughes, *Robert Hall (1764–1831)* (London: Independent Press Ltd., 1961); George J. Griffin, "Robert Hall's Contribution to Early Baptist Missions," *Baptist History and Heritage*, 3, No.1 (January, 1968): 3–8, 42; Thomas R. McKibbens, Jr., *The Forgotten Heritage: A Lineage of Great Baptist Preaching* (Macon, Georgia: Mercer University Press, 1986), 61–66.

16 *Reflections on the Character and State of Departed Christians* (Birmingham: J. Belcher, 1791). For a selection from this sermon, see pages 71–75 ("Friendship to Christ").

17 A collier is a coal miner.

for interrupting sighs and sobs."[18] Preaching on the cross would become a central theme in Pearce's pulpit ministry.

Finally, there was the rich fellowship to be enjoyed with fellow students. Two students in particular became close friends, Josiah Evans (1760–1792), who never finished his studies at the Academy owing to ill-health,[19] and William Steadman (1764–1837), who was later to play a central role in Baptist renewal and theological education in the North of England.[20] Steadman's son later recounted how Pearce, Steadman and Evans used to meet together two or three times a week for "perusal of the Scriptures, and prayer."[21]

## *"For God's glory"*

Early in 1789, Pearce received and accepted a call to serve for a year's probation as the pastor of Cannon Street Baptist Church in the centre of Birmingham.[22] Pearce had supplied the Birmingham pulpit the previous summer as well as over the Christmas vacation. Impressed by Pearce's evangelistic zeal—a number were saved on both occasions—along with his ability to edify God's people, the church sent their request to him in early February 1789. Five weeks later Pearce wrote back consenting to their request, and by June, his studies finished, he was with them.[23] The following year

---

18 Cited S. Pearce Carey, *Samuel Pearce M.A., The Baptist Brainerd* (3rd ed.; London: The Carey Press, [c.1922]), 83.

19 On Josiah Evans, see page 79–82.

20 On the life and ministry of Steadman, see Thomas Steadman, *Memoir of the Rev. William Steadman, D.D.* (London: Thomas Ward and Co., 1838); Sharon James, "William Steadman (1764–1837) in Michael A.G. Haykin, ed., *The British Particular Baptists, 1638–1910* (Springfield, Missouri: Particular Baptist Press, 2000), II, 162–181.

21 Steadman, *Memoir of the Rev. William Steadman*, 37.

22 For the early history of the Cannon Street congregation, see J.E. Hale, *Cannon Street Baptist Church, Birmingham. Its History from 1737 to 1880, with Some Account of Its Pastors* (London: Elliot Stock/Birmingham: Hudson & Son, 1880).

23 Carey, *Samuel Pearce*, 93–94.

he was formally called to be the pastor of what would turn out to be his only pastoral charge. In his letter of acceptance, written on July 18, 1790, he told the Birmingham Baptists that he hoped the union between pastor and church would "be for God's glory, for the good of precious souls, for your prosperity as a Church, and for my prosperity as your minister."[24] It should be noted that he placed "God's glory" in first place. If there was any concern that set the fundamental tone for his ministry, it was this desire to see God glorified in his life and labours. It is also noteworthy that he asked to be given a yearly holiday of six weeks so that he could visit his father in Plymouth.[25] A few days later, on July 25, 1790, his home church in Plymouth wrote a letter of dismissal to Pearce for their sister congregation in Birmingham. In it, Pearce was told, "You have a great harvest of souls in prospect." Among the deacons who signed it was Pearce's father.[26]

His ministry at Cannon Street occupied ten all-too-brief years. Yet, they were ones of tremendous activity and great fruitfulness, which laid the foundations for the congregation's remarkable growth in the early nineteenth century. He regularly preached three times on the Lord's Day and usually in neighbouring villages two or three times during the week.[27] No less than 335 individuals were converted under his ministry and received into the membership of Cannon Street. This figure does not include those converted

---

24 Cited Carey, *Samuel Pearce*, 95.

25 Samuel Pearce, Letter to Cannon Street Baptist Church, July 10, 1790, in "Cannon Street Memorial Baptist Church Minute Book, 1778–1798" (Birmingham City Archives, Birmingham, England), entry for July 11, 1790. See also Carey, *Samuel Pearce*, 48–49.

26 Philip Gibbs and Deacons of the Baptist Church in Plymouth, Letter of Dismissal, July 25, 1790 ("Volume containing correspondence, plans, insurance policies, legal documents, trust deeds, wills, etc. [of Cannon Street Baptist Church]," Birmingham City Archives, Birmingham, BC2 [Acc. 91/62]/61).

27 William Ward, Letter, January 5, 1799 (Fuller, *Memoirs of the Rev. Samuel Pearce*, 139).

under his preaching who, for one reason or another, did not join themselves to the Birmingham cause.[28] In 1793 Pearce told the American Baptist William Rogers (1751–1824) that

> scarce a Sabbath has passed, or a sermon been preached without a peculiar blessing attending it, both to the consolation of the righteous, and the conversion of sinners. We rejoice with trembling. Hitherto indeed we have the happiness of seeing every individual who has been added to us, so walk as to adorn the holy religion of the Son of God; and notwithstanding the painful vicissitudes which frequently follow on unusual revivals, our hopes still predominate.[29]

It bears noting that ministry in the town was not easy. By the 1790s Birmingham had become the leading industrial centre of the Midlands and the largest industrial town in England after London. Many visitors were impressed by the prosperity evident in certain quarters of the town, but the Romantic poet Robert Southey (1774–1843) noted the cost of the industrialization when he commented after a visit to Birmingham in 1802:

> I am still giddy, dizzied with the hammering of presses, the clatter of engines and the whirling of wheels; my head aches with the multiplicity of infernal noises, and my eyes

---

28 Carey, *Samuel Pearce*, 113; Arthur S. Langley, *Birmingham Baptists: Past and Present* (London: The Kingsgate Press, 1939), 34. Even after Pearce's death, his wife Sarah could rejoice in people joining the church who had been saved under her husband's ministry. See [Andrew Fuller?], "Memoir of Mrs. Pearce," *The Theological and Biblical Magazine*, 5 (1805): 7. For some of her letters, see pages 201–217.

29 Letter to William Rogers, January 14, 1793 ("Extracts from two Letters from the Rev. S. Pearce, of Birmingham, to the Rev. Dr. Rogers, of Philadelphia, dated Sept. 3, 1792, and Jan. 14, 1793," *The Massachusetts Baptist Missionary Magazine*, 1 [1807]: 299).

with the light of infernal fires,—I may add, my heart also,
at the sight of so many human beings employed in infernal
occupations and looking as if they were never destined for
anything better. ...Think not, however, that I am insensible
to the wonders of the place:—in no other age or country
was there ever so astonishing a display of human ingenuity:
but watch-chains, necklaces and bracelets, buttons, buckles
and snuff-boxes are dearly purchased at the expense of
health and morality and...it must be confessed that human
reason has more cause at present for humiliation than for
triumph at Birmingham.[30]

And when Isaiah Birt, through whose preaching Pearce had been
converted, visited Pearce three years after the latter had settled in
the town, he noted that the country around the town was one of
"burning, of smoke, and of terror," filled as it was with "engines
and...fires...in the coal and iron works."[31] The majority of the
Cannon Street congregation were drawn from those who laboured
in these iron works and factories, and had done so since they were
young children. The result was that many of them were, in Pearce's
words, "unable to repeat [even] the alphabet" when they first came
to the church.[32] A Sunday School was thus started in 1795 and
within a very short period of time grew to the point that some 200
scholars were enrolled in it. Pearce was quite active in this venture,
teaching "the principles of religion, natural philosophy, [and]
astronomy."[33] Pearce also oversaw the establishment of a "benevo-

30 [Robert Southey], *Letters from England* (2nd ed.; London: Longman, Hurst,
Rees and Orme, 1808), II, 56–57, 59–60.

31 Isaiah Birt, Diary, June 7, 1792 (John Birt, "Memoir of the Late Rev. Isaiah
Birt," *The Baptist Magazine*, 30 [1838]: 107).

32 Letter to William Rogers, January 27, 1794, "Original Letters, of the Rev.
Samuel Pearce," *The Religious Remembrancer* (October 8, 1814): 22.

33 William Ward, Letter, January 5, 1799 (Fuller, *Memoirs of the Rev. Samuel Pearce*,
139).

lent society," which provided forty to fifty pounds a year to help the poor in the congregation, as well as the founding of "a sick society for visiting the afflicted in general."[34] Not long after Pearce's death the church building was enlarged to seat 900. And by the 1830s, the congregation had become the second largest Baptist cause in the British Isles. Pearce was also active in preaching in some of the villages around Birmingham, including Shirley, Kingswood, Wythall, Cradley and Bromsgrove, where a number of churches resulted from his evangelism.[35]

Given both the blessings and challenges of Pearce's ministry, it should occasion no surprise to find that he spent long hours involved in ministry. In fact, the London Baptist John Rippon (1751–1836) speaks of him labouring "eighteen hours" a day. While this remark is definitely an exaggeration, nevertheless it does reflect the intensity with which Pearce poured himself into his ministry.[36] It is noteworthy in this regard that in the only published ordination sermon of Pearce, one that he preached on Ephesians 4:11 at the ordination of William Belsher, the pastor of the Baptist cause in Worcester, Pearce admonished his hearers to respect the time their pastor needed for study:

---

34 William Ward, Letter, January 5, 1799 (Fuller, *Memoirs of the Rev. Samuel Pearce*, 139).

35 For details of Pearce's ministry in these towns and villages, see James Ford, "A Historical Sketch of the Midland Baptist Association" in J. Gwynne Owen, *Records of an Old Association* (N.p.: n.p., 1905), 106–107; Alan Betteridge, *Deep Roots, Living Branches: A History of Baptists in the English Western Midlands* (Kibworth Beauchamp, Leicester: Matador, 2010), 90–91.

36 See Rippon, *Baptist Annual Register*, 3:34, note, where the London Baptist speaks of Pearce's "pen…[having] been long in daily career eighteen hours together." Fuller does mention that Pearce was in the habit of staying up studying till two or three in the morning (*Memoirs of the Rev. Samuel Pearce*, 64, note ★). However, Fuller also mentioned that early in his ministry Pearce engaged in "bodily exercise" as a way of relaxation. In his final years, he would relax by means of scientific experimentation with a microscope (Fuller, *Memoirs of the Rev. Samuel Pearce*, 205).

I want to convince you that, for your own sakes, you should promote a studious habit in your minister; allow him every inch of time he wants; neither call upon him, nor expect him to call upon you for no better purpose than to gossip; especially let his *mornings* and his *Saturdays* be sacred—it is little short of cruelty to interrupt him then. As you love him, so, no doubt, you will feel a pleasure in his company; but let him choose his own times for seeing you; and do not accuse him of criminal negligence, if his visits are less frequent than you expect. Perhaps at the very moment of your disappointment, he was studying something against the Lord's Day for your case—perhaps at the moment you are censuring him for his neglect, he is wrestling with God for you in his closet![37]

Here Pearce surely speaks from personal experience of the tension that pastors in the Protestant tradition have repeatedly faced: the need to devote substantial time to sermon-preparation and prayer while also caring for the souls of those in their churches.[38] The strength of language that Pearce uses here—"little short of cruelty" and "criminal negligence"—definitely indicates that this issue is

---

37 John Ryland, Jr. and Samuel Pearce, *The Duty of Ministers to be Nursing Fathers to the Church; and the Duty of Churches To Regard Ministers as the Gift of Christ* (London, 1796), 51–52. Italics in the original.

For a brief overview of Belsher's ministry in Worcester, see William Urwick, *Nonconformity in Worcester* (London: Simpkin, Marshall, Hamilton, Kent & Co., 1897), 151–152. When Belsher came to Worcester in 1796, the membership of the church stood at 24. Within a relatively short period of time, "by the blessing of God" on the preaching of the Word, the membership had quadrupled to 96 (Joseph Ivimey, *A History of the English Baptists* [London: Isaac Taylor Hinton and Holdsworth & Ball, 1830], IV, 548–549).

38 On the importance of pastoral visitation in Pearce's Calvinistic Baptist tradition, see Nigel David Wheeler, "Eminent Spirituality and Eminent Usefulness: Andrew Fuller's (1754–1815) Pastoral Theology in his Ordination Sermons" (Unpublished Ph.D. thesis, University of Pretoria, 2009), 152–154.

no minor matter for Pearce. In fact, was Pearce thinking that such an encouragement to the congregation might spare Belsher problems that he himself had experienced?

At the heart of Pearce's preaching and spirituality was that keynote of evangelicalism, the mercy of God displayed in the cross of Christ. Writing one Sunday afternoon to William Summers, a close friend then residing in London, Pearce told him that he had for his sermon that evening

> the best subject of all in the Bible. Eph. i.7—Redemption! how welcome to the captive! Forgiveness! how delightful to the guilty! Grace! how pleasant to the heart of a saved sinner!" Christ's atoning death for sinners, he went on to say, is "the leading truth in the N.T.,...a doctrine I cannot but venerate; and to the Author of such a redemption my whole soul labours to exhaust itself in praise."[39]

In his final letter to his congregation, written on May 31, 1799, he reminded them that the gospel, which he had preached among them for ten years and in which he urged them to stand fast, was "the gospel of the grace of God; the gospel of free, full, everlasting salvation, founded on the sufferings and death of God manifest in the flesh."[40]

Men and women called him the "silver-tongued" because of the intensity and power of his preaching.[41] John Ryland, Jr. (1753–1825), one of his closest friends, reckoned that he and Benjamin Francis (1734–1799), who wrote an elegy for Pearce, were the "two most

---

39 Cited Carey, *Samuel Pearce*, 97–98.

40 Fuller, *Memoirs of the Rev. Samuel Pearce*, 153–154. For the rest of this letter, see pages 193–195. See also his funeral sermon for Caleb Evans, where he describes "the doctrine of the Atonement" as "that great leading truth of the gospel" (*Reflections on the Character and State of Departed Christians*, 16).

41 Payne, "Samuel Pearce," 48–49.

popular preachers" among the Baptist community of their day.[42] From one perspective, the blessing of God on his ministry was due, in part, to his exaltation of the crucified Christ as noted above, for God the Father ever blesses such honouring of his Son. From another perspective, it was because Pearce was deeply conscious of his need for the anointing of the Holy Spirit on his public ministry.[43] At the outset of the short ministry of Joseph Swain (1761–1796) at Walworth in 1792, for example, Pearce observed to him: "Brother Swain, you preach Christ sweetly, but remember if you are successful it must be by the blessing of the Holy Ghost. Pray honor the Holy Ghost."[44]

But there were times when preaching was a real struggle for him. Writing to William Carey (1761–1834) in August 1796, for example, he told the Baptist missionary who at that time was living in Mudnabati, West Bengal:

> At some times, I question whether I ever knew the grace of God in truth; and at others I hesitate on the most important points of Christian faith. I have lately had peculiar struggles of this kind with my own heart, and have often half concluded to speak no more in the name of the Lord. When I am preparing for the pulpit, I fear I am going to avow fables for facts and doctrines of men for the truths of God. In conversation I am obliged to be silent, lest my tongue should belie my heart. In prayer I know not what

---

42 *The Work of Faith, the Labour of Love, and the Patience of Hope Illustrated; in the Life and Death of the Reverend Andrew Fuller* (London: Button & Son, 1816), 226. For Francis' elegy, see *An Elegy on the Death of the Rev. Samuel Pearce, A.M.* (Bristol, 1799).

43 This was the observation of John Ryland in his funeral sermon for Pearce: *The promised presence of Christ with his People a source of Consolation under the most painful Bereavements* (Clipstone: J.W. Morris, 1799), 50.

44 "The London Association of Strict Baptist Ministers and Churches," *The Primitive Church Magazine*, 6, n.s. (1849): 231. On Swain, see Ivimey, *History of the English Baptists*, IV, 400–403.

to say, and at times think prayer altogether useless. Yet I cannot wholly surrender my hope, or my profession.— Three things I find, above all others, tend to my preservation:—First, a recollection of time when, at once, I was brought to abandon the practice of sins which the fear of damnation could never bring me to relinquish before. Surely, I say, this must be the finger of God, according to the Scripture doctrine of regeneration:—Second, I feel such a consciousness of guilt that nothing but the gospel scheme can satisfy my mind respecting the hope of salvation: and, Thirdly, I see that what true devotion does appear in the world, seems only to be found among those to whom Christ is precious.[45]

Moreover, there were some in the congregation who did not appreciate his pulpit ministry. One such individual was a certain John Smith, who, in April 1795 publicly accused Pearce of anti-Scriptural teaching. Smith may well have been an Antinomian, for there is an indication that in the early days of his ministry at Cannon Street, Pearce had to deal with Antinomianism. The Birmingham pastor told his American correspondent William Rogers, for example, in January 1794, that there were some in his congregation who had been drawn to what Pearce called "an injudicious ministry." In their zeal for doctrine, they had forgotten that the Lord Jesus "gave himself for us to purchase to himself a peculiar people *zealous for good works*."[46] Smith himself was censured at a church meeting

45 Fuller, *Memoirs of the Rev. Samuel Pearce*, 104–105. For Pearce's convictions regarding "the best mode of preaching," see "Extracts from a Letter of the Late Mr. Pearce to a Young Minister just Before his Ordination," *The Baptist Magazine*, 1 (1809): 361–362. For William Carey, see page 27, note 87.

46 Letter to William Rogers, January 27, 1794. As Pearce rightly noted in a sermon he preached on Psalm 55:6 in May 1792, the true child of God "loves holiness, and pants after it" ("Sketch of a Sermon by the Late Rev. S. Pearce, of Birmingham," *The Baptist Magazine*, 32 [1840]: 237). See also pages 95–106 ("On doing good").

since he had also been speaking to other members of the congregation, seeking to turn them against Pearce. Within a month Smith had repented. The issue of whether or not his repentance was real, however, dragged on for the rest of the year.[47]

Early in Pearce's ministry there was also a sad separation involving a member by the name of Joseph Belcher (c.1767–1816), who believed he was called to pastoral ministry, but the leadership of Cannon Street demurred. Belcher could not shake this conviction and eventually left in January 1792, whereupon he joined the other Baptist congregation that met in Birmingham on Bond Street. In 1795 he was called to pastor the Baptist cause in Rushden, Northamptonshire, where he enjoyed significant blessing on his ministry.[48] Pearce was a remarkably godly man, but, as this incident reveals, piety does not bestow infallibility. Thankfully, some of the Belcher family stayed in the Cannon Street congregation, one of whom, also named Joseph Belcher (1794–1859) played a significant role in the printing of the works of Pearce's first biographer, Andrew Fuller.[49]

Only a handful of Pearce's sermons were ever published. The earliest is a sermon he preached during the heady days of the early 1790s when it seemed that the remnants of the Clarendon Code, legislation passed during the Restoration to suppress Nonconformity, would be repealed.[50] There is a funeral sermon for his Bristol mentor, Caleb Evans;[51] a sermon on baptism based on Acts

---

47 "Cannon Street Memorial Baptist Church Minute Book, 1794–1801" (Birmingham City Archives, Birmingham, England), entries for April 23, 1795; May 23, 1795; November 12, 1795; and November 26, 1795.

48 J[oseph] B[elcher], "Memoir of Mr. Joseph Belcher," *The Baptist Magazine*, 8 (1816): 353–356.

49 See page 202.

50 *The oppressive, unjust, and prophane Nature, and Tendency of the Corporation and Test Acts, exposed* (Birmingham: J. Thompson, 1790).

51 *Reflections on the Character and State of Departed Christians.*

28:22;[52] an ordination sermon on Ephesians 4:11;[53] a sermon preached in London at the Little Prescot Street Baptist meeting-house in support of a London Sunday School;[54] and a thanksgiving sermon for two British naval victories in 1798.[55]

There are also two circular letters for the Midland Baptist Association that Pearce drew up in 1794 and 1795 that dealt respectively with the subjects of doing good and salvation solely by God's free grace.[56] A good perspective on his thought as it pertains to soteriology may be found in the following extract from the latter circular letter:

> The point of difference between us and many other professing Christians lies in the doctrine of salvation entirely by grace. For whilst some assert that good works are the cause of justification; some that good works are united with the merits of Christ and so both contribute to our justification; and others that good works neither in whole nor in part justify, but the act of faith; we renounce everything in point of our acceptance with God, but his free Grace alone which justifies the ungodly, still treading in the steps of our venerable forefathers, the compilers of the Baptist Confession of Faith, who thus express themselves

---

52 *The Scripture Doctrine of Christian Baptism; with Some Historical Remarks on That Subject* (1794 ed.; repr. Birmingham, 1806).

53 *The Duty of Churches To Regard Ministers as the Gift of Christ* in his and John Ryland, Jr., *The Duty of Ministers To Be Nursing Fathers to the Church; and the Duty of Churches To Regard Ministers as the Gift of Christ*, 40–64.

54 *An Early Acquaintance with the Holy Scriptures Recommended* (Clipstone: J.W. Morris, 1800).

55 *Motives of Gratitude* (Birmingham: James Belcher, [1798]).

56 *Doing Good* (Circular Letter of the Midland Association, 1794, in William Stokes, *The History of the Midland Association of Baptist Churches, from Its Rise in the Year 1655 to 1855* [London: R. Theobald/Birmingham: John W. Showell, 1855], 115–121) and *The Doctrine of Salvation by Free Grace Alone* (1795 ed.; repr. n.p.: New York Baptist Association, 1855). See pages 95–106 and 131–145 for these texts.

respecting the doctrine of justification: "Those whom God effectually calleth, he also freely justifieth,...for Christ's sake alone; not by imputing faith itself, the act of believing, or any other evangelical obedience to them as their righteousness; but by imputing Christ's active obedience unto the whole law, and passive obedience in his death for their whole and sole righteousness, they receiving and resting on him and his righteousness by faith" which "is the alone instrument of justification."[57]

In this point do all the other lines of our confession meet. For if it be admitted that justification is an act of free grace in God without any respect to the merit or demerit of the person justified, then the doctrines of Jehovah's sovereign love in choosing to himself a people from before the foundation of the world, his sending his Son to *expiate* their guilt, his effectual operations upon their hearts, and his perfecting the work he has begun in them until those whom he justifies he also glorifies, will be embraced as necessary parts of the glorious scheme of our salvation.[58]

## "My invaluable Sarah"

A vital support to Pearce throughout his pastorate at Cannon Street was his closest friend, his wife Sarah. A third-generation Baptist whose father was a deacon,[59] Sarah Hopkins (1771–1804) had met Pearce soon after his arrival in Birmingham and appears to have

---

57 *The Second London Confession of Faith* 11.1, 2.

58 *Salvation by Free Grace Alone*, 2. For a succinct statement of Pearce's doctrinal convictions, see also Samuel Pearce's Confession of Faith on pages 55–60.

59 Her father was Joshua Hopkins (d.1798), a grocer and a deacon in Alcester Baptist Church, Warwickshire, for close to thirty years. Her maternal grandfather was John Ash (1724–1779), pastor of the Baptist cause in Pershore, Worcestershire, and a noteworthy Baptist minister of the eighteenth century.

been converted under his preaching.[60] Pearce was soon deeply in love with Sarah, and she with him. As he wrote to her on December 24, 1790, about the impact her letters had on him:

> Were I averse to writing,…one of your dear Epistles could not fail of conquering the antipathy and transforming it into desire. The moment I peruse a line from my Sarah, I am inspired at the propensity which never leaves me, till I have thrown open my whole heart, and returned a copy of it to the dear being who long since compelled it to a *voluntary surrender,* and whose claims have never since been disputed.[61]

They were married on February 2, 1791. With delight, Pearce wrote the following day to a friend of his and Sarah's:

> The occasion of my writing is a source of joy inexpressible to myself—a joy in which I know you will participate. I am no longer a bachelor. Your amiable friend permitted me to call her my own yesterday. One dwelling now contains us both, and Paul's Square contains that dwelling.[62]

Later that same year, during November, she was baptized by her husband.[63]

---

60 "Memoir of Mrs. Pearce," 1.

61 Letter to Sarah Hopkins, December 24, 1790 (Pearce-Carey Correspondence 1790–1828, Angus Library, Regent's Park College, University of Oxford). For the rest of this letter, see pages 65–67.

62 Letter, February 3, 1791 (cited Joseph Belcher, "The Wife of Samuel Pearce," *The Mothers Journal and Family Visitant*, 19 [1854]: 12). St Paul's Square, so-named because of the Anglican church at its centre, contains probably the finest example of surviving Georgian architecture in Birmingham today. In Pearce's day, its architectural elegance made it a much-sought-after locale in which to live.

63 "Memoir of Mrs. Pearce," 1.

Pearce's understanding of what should lie at the heart of their marriage found expression in a letter that he wrote to his future wife a little over two months before their wedding: "may my dear Sarah & myself be made the means of leading each other on in the way to the heavenly kingdom & at last there meet to know what even temporary separation means no more."[64] Husband and wife are to be a means of grace to one another in their earthly pilgrimage. In that joint pilgrimage, they are to be, as a recent book on marriage has put it, "intimate allies."[65]

One sees the way in which Pearce sought to help his wife spiritually in the following passage from a letter written on December 2, 1791: "I trust this will find you expecting a good Sabbath & waiting for the day of the Lord with ardent desires after his tabernacle—may your enjoyments equal your desires."[66] He then went on to give his wife some advice about conversing with a Mrs. Briggs, who appears to have imbibed Socinianism. He told Sarah:

> avoid any religious controversy with Mrs Briggs—I fear she has more studied system than yielded herself to the influence of truth—you my love I believe have been better employed...I have been much afraid lest she should distress your mind—I am under no apprehensions of her altering your sentiments—I believe you have been taught them by the Holy Ghost who dwelleth in you—& that you will be kept therein by the power of God—but it will pain your mind to hear your Lord degraded & the

64 Letter to Sarah Hopkins, November 26, 1790 (Samuel Pearce Carey Collection-Pearce Family Letters, Angus Library, Regent's Park College, University of Oxford).

65 Dan B. Allender and Tremper Longman III, *Intimate Allies* (Carol Stream, Illinois: Tyndale House, 1995).

66 Letter to Sarah Pearce, December 2, 1791 (Samuel Pearce Mss., FPC D55, Angus Library, Regent's Park College, University of Oxford).

blood wherewith you were sanctified accounted an unholy thing. [67]

In another letter, this one written from Northampton, where he
had gone to preach for John Ryland, he encouraged Sarah in a
postscript: "Let us both live near to God & our separation from
each other will be the less regretted—O be much in prayer for
your own S.P."[68]

Pearce's love for his wife clearly deepened with the passing of
the years. In 1791, only a couple of months after their wedding, he
told her that he was more desirous "of enjoying *your* friendship
than the admiration of crowds of Helen's, or Venus's, or Cleopatra's,
or all the females of *Egypt—Greece—Rome* or *Birmingham*."[69] He
concluded this letter by telling her: "when I add all the *respect*, the
*gratitude*, the *tenderness*, & *affection* of which my nature is capable
into *one sum*—I feel the whole comes vastly short of what I owe
to *you* my lovely friend! My inestimable Sarah!"[70] In a letter that is
undated but that was probably written in early 1792, Pearce concluded it by telling Sarah, "O that you were now within these
longing arms & then there would be no occasion to write to your
more than ever affectionate S. Pearce."[71] And writing on a preaching
trip to Wales in July of 1792, he told his wife, "How often have I
longed for your Society since I left you…every pleasant scene
which opened to us on our way (& they were very numerous) lost
half its beauty because my lovely Sarah was not present to partake
its pleasures with me." He had to remind himself, though, "to see
the country was not the immediate object of my visiting Wales—I
came to preach the gospel—to tell poor sinners of the dear Lord

67 Letter to Sarah Pearce, December 2, 1791 (Samuel Pearce Mss.).
68 Letter to Sarah Pearce, August 23, 1792 (Samuel Pearce Mss.).
69 Letter to Sarah Pearce, April 1, 1791 (Samuel Pearce Mss.).
70 Letter to Sarah Pearce, April 1, 1791 (Samuel Pearce Mss.).
71 Letter to Sarah Pearce (Samuel Pearce Mss.).

Jesus—to endeavor to restore the children of misery to the pious pleasures of divine enjoyment."[72]

Again, when his wife was away on a trip to Shropshire, Samuel wrote: "I feel myself such a poor dull solitary thing without you that I fly to my pen that I may at least feel some relief in writing to the dearest Friend I have whilst I am deprived the felicity of her presence and conversation." Three and a half years after their marriage, he wrote to her from Plymouth: "O, my Sarah, had I as much proof of my love to Christ as I have of my love to you, I should prize it above rubies."[73] When Pearce was away from his wife the following year, 1795, on a preaching trip in London, he wrote to tell her,

> every day improves not only my tenderness but my *esteem* for you. Called as I now am to mingle much with society in all its orders I have daily opportunity of making re- marks on human temper & after all I have seen and thought my *judgement* as well as my *affection* still approves of *you* as the *best of women* for *me*.[74]

On the same trip he called her "the dearest of women—my invalu- able Sarah."[75] In another letter written about the same time he informed the one whom he called the "partner of my heart" that his letter was a "forerunner of her impatient husband who weary with so long an absence"—he had obviously been away from home for a few weeks—"[longs] again to embrace his dearest

---

72 Letter to Sarah Pearce, July 11, 1792 (Samuel Pearce Mss.).

73 S. Pearce Carey, "Love Letters of Samuel Pearce," *The Baptist Quarterly*, 8 (1936–1937): 96. In his biography of Pearce, Carey has a slightly different version of this quote. Carey appears to have "modernized" the sentence for the biography; see Carey, *Samuel Pearce*, 122.

74 Letter to Sarah Pearce, September 7, 1795 (Samuel Pearce Mss.).

75 Letter to Sarah Pearce, August 31, 1795 (Samuel Pearce Mss.).

friend."[76] The following year, when he was involved in an extensive preaching trip in Ireland, he wrote to his wife from Dublin on June 24:

> last evening…were my eyes delighted at the sight of a letter from my dear Sarah…I rejoice that you, as well as myself, find that "absence diminishes not affection." For my part I compare our present correspondence to a kind of courtship, rendered sweeter than what usually bears that name by a *certainty of success*…. Not less than when I sought your hand [in marriage], do I *now* court your heart, nor doth the *security* of possessing you at all lessen my pleasure at the prospect of calling you my own, when we meet again.

And then toward the end of the letter he added:

> O our dear fireside! When shall we sit down toe to toe, and tete á tete [*sic*] again—Not a long time I hope will elapse ere I re-enjoy that felicity.[77]

That Sarah felt the same toward Samuel is seen in a letter she wrote after her husband's death to her sister Rebecca. Rebecca had just been married to a Mr. Harris and Sarah prayed that she might "enjoy the most uninterrupted Happiness…(for indeed I can scarce form an idia [*sic*]…this side of Heaven of greater) equal to what *I have* enjoyed."[78] It is a shame that none of Sarah's letters to Samuel have survived, though Sarah did admit she had "a natural disinclination" to writing letters,[79] which may mean that there was

76 Letter to Sarah Pearce, September 7, 1795 (Samuel Pearce Mss.).
77 Letter to Sarah Pearce, June 24, 1796 (Samuel Pearce Mss.).
78 Letter to Rebecca Harris, March 29, 1800 (Samuel Pearce Mss.).
79 Sarah Pearce, Letter to William Rogers, June 16, 1801 ("Original Letters, of

considerably less correspondence from her to Samuel than there was from him to her.

One final word about Samuel and Sarah's marriage needs to be said. What especially delighted Pearce about his wife was her Christian piety. For example, he told Sarah in the summer of 1793 in response to a letter he had received from her: "I cannot convey to you an idea of the holy rapture I felt at the account you gave me of your soul prosperity."[80] Close friends of Sarah noted that since her conversion she had had "a strong attachment to evangelical truth" and "a longing desire for the universal spread of the gospel."[81] And by her own admission, she was "deeply interested in all that interested" Samuel.[82]

## "I will find a sermon"

One leading characteristic of Pearce's spirituality has already been noted, namely, its crucicentrism. "Christ crucified," his good friend Andrew Fuller wrote of him, "was his darling theme, from first to last."[83] Another prominent feature of his spirituality was a passion for the salvation of his fellow human beings. This passion is strikingly revealed in four events.

The first took place when Pearce was asked to preach at the opening of a Baptist meeting-house in Guilsborough, Northamptonshire,

the Rev. Samuel Pearce," *The Religious Remembrancer* [October 1, 1814]: 19).

80 Letter to Sarah Pearce, June 14, 1793 (Samuel Pearce Mss.). See also Letter [to William Summers?], October 26, 1790, in ["Extracts from Mr. Pearce's Letters"], *The Baptist Magazine*, 1 (1809): 56, where Pearce mentions visiting Sarah before their marriage and having a discussion on "the subject of experimental, heart religion." Pearce was thrilled to find that Sarah "was no stranger to it."

81 "Memoir of Mrs. Pearce," 1–2.

82 Sarah Pearce, Letter to William Rogers, June 16, 1801.

83 Fuller, *Memoirs of the Rev. Samuel Pearce*, 191. For crucicentrism as a distinctive characteristic of eighteenth-century evangelicalism, see also David Bebbington, *Evangelicalism in Modern Britain. A History from the 1730s to the 1980s* (1989 ed.; repr. Grand Rapids: Baker Book House, 1992), 14–17.

on Wednesday, May 7, 1794. The previous meeting-house had been burned down at Christmas, 1792, by a mob that was hostile to Baptists.[84] Pearce had spoken in the morning on Psalm 76:10 ("Surely the wrath of man shall praise thee: the remainder of wrath shalt thou restrain.").[85] Later that day, during the midday meal, it was quite evident from the conversation at the dinner tables that Pearce's sermon had been warmly appreciated. It was thus no surprise when Pearce was asked if he would be willing to preach again the following morning. "If you will find a congregation," Pearce responded, "I will find a sermon." It was agreed to have the sermon at 5 A.M. so that a number of farm labourers who wanted to hear Pearce preach could come and still be at their tasks early in the morning.

After Pearce had preached the second time—and that to a congregation of more than 200 people—and was sitting at breakfast with a few others, including Andrew Fuller, the latter remarked to Pearce how pleased he had been with the content of his friend's sermon. But, he went on to say, it seemed to him that Pearce's sermon was poorly structured. "I thought," Fuller told his friend, "you did not seem to close when you had really finished. I wondered that, contrary to what is usual with you, you seemed, as it were, to begin again at the end—how was it?" Pearce's response was terse: "It was so; but I had my reason." "Well then, come, let us have it," Fuller jovially responded. Pearce was quite reluctant to divulge the reason, but after a further entreaty from Fuller, he consented and said:

> Well, my brother, you shall have the secret, if it must be so. Just at the moment I was about to resume my seat, thinking I had finished, the door opened, and I saw a poor man

---

84 For the details, see John Rippon, *The Baptist Annual Register* (London, 1794–1797), 2:9–10, note.

85 For a letter in which Pearce mentions some of the details surrounding this event, see pages 92–94.

enter, of the working class; and from the sweat on his brow, and the symptoms of his fatigue, I conjectured that he had walked some miles to this early service, but that he had been unable to reach the place till the close. A momentary thought glanced through my mind—here may be a man who never heard the gospel, or it may be he is one that regards it as a feast of fat things; in either case, the effort on his part demands one on mine. So with the hope of doing him good, I resolved at once to forget all else, and, in despite of criticism, and the apprehension of being thought tedious, to give him a quarter of an hour.[86]

As Fuller and the others present at the breakfast table listened to this simple explanation, they were deeply impressed by Pearce's evident love for souls. Not afraid to appear as one lacking in homiletical skill, especially in the eyes of his fellow pastors, Pearce's zeal for the spiritual health of *all* his hearers had led him to minister as best he could to this "poor man" who had arrived late.

---

86 Cox, *History of the Baptist Missionary Society*, I, 52–53. Pearce's friendship with Fuller drew him into a highly significant circle of friends. For the story of this circle, see Michael A.G. Haykin, *One Heart and One Soul: John Sutcliff of Olney, His Friends and His Times* (Darlington, Co. Durham: Evangelical Press, 1994).

Andrew Fuller was the pre-eminent English-speaking Baptist theologian of his day. For his life and ministry, see the classic study by his friend, John Ryland, Jr., *The Work of Faith, the Labour of Love, and the Patience of Hope Illustrated; in the Life and Death of the Reverend Andrew Fuller* (London: Button & Son, 1816). A second edition of this biography appeared in 1818. For more recent studies, see Gilbert S. Laws, *Andrew Fuller: Pastor, Theologian, Ropeholder* (London: Carey Press, 1942); Peter J. Morden, *Offering Christ to the World: Andrew Fuller (1754–1815) and the Revival of Eighteenth-Century Particular Baptist Life* (Carlisle, Cumbria, U.K./Waynesboro, Georgia: Paternoster Press, 2003) and Paul Brewster, *Andrew Fuller: Model Pastor-Theologian* (Nashville, Tennessee: B&H Publishing, 2010). On his thought, see also Michael A. G. Haykin, ed., *'At the Pure Fountain of Thy Word': Andrew Fuller as an Apologist* (Carlisle, Cumbria, U.K./Waynesboro, Georgia: Paternoster Press, 2004), and for his piety, see Michael A.G. Haykin, *The Armies of the Lamb: The Spirituality of Andrew Fuller* (Dundas, Ontario: Joshua Press, 2001).

# *"An inﬅrument of establishing the empire of my dear Lord"*

Given his ardour for the advance of the gospel it is only to be expected that Pearce would be vitally involved in the formation, in October 1792, of what would eventually be termed the Baptist Missionary Society, the womb of the modern missionary movement.[87] The week after the formation of this society, Pearce preached a sermon to his own congregation on the necessity of Christians exerting themselves in the cause of missions. As he put it two years later: "A Christian's heart ought to be as comprehensive as the universe. The Asiatic, the American, and the African, as well as the European, have a claim on your philanthropy."[88] In fact, by that same year, 1794, Pearce was so gripped by the cause of missions that he had arrived at the conviction that he should offer his services to the Society and go out to India to join the first

---

87 On the emergence of this missionary society, see Haykin, *One Heart and One Soul*, 198–235. The most well-known figure associated with the early history of this society was, of course, William Carey, who has been briefly mentioned above. The story of how Carey, a cobbler by training, became the learned father of the modern missionary movement is a well-known one to Baptists and has rightly become central to their thinking about the nature of Baptist identity. He and Pearce probably first met in early 1791 and they became fast friends.

On Carey's life, the classic studies are those by his nephew and great-grandson: Eustace Carey, *Memoir of William Carey, D.D.* (London: Jackson and Walford, 1836) and Samuel Pearce Carey, *William Carey* (8th ed.; London: The Carey Press, 1934). Other important studies include George Smith, *The Life of William Carey: Shoemaker & Missionary* (London: J.M. Dent & Sons/New York: E.P. Dutton, 1909); Mary Drewery, *William Carey: Shoemaker and Missionary* (London: Hodder and Stoughton, 1978); Timothy George, *Faithful Witness: The Life and Mission of William Carey* (Birmingham, Alabama: New Hope, 1991); Keith Farrer, *William Carey: Missionary and Botanist* (Kew, Victoria, Australia: Carey Baptist Grammar School, 2005); and John Appleby, *'I Can Plod…': William Carey and the Early Years of the First Baptist Missionary Society* (London: Grace Publications Trust, 2007).

88 See page 104.

missionary team the Society had sent out, namely, William Carey, John Thomas (1757–1801) and their respective families. He began to study Bengali on his own.[89] For the entire month of October 1794, which preceded the early November meeting of the Society's administrative committee, where Pearce's offer would be evaluated, Pearce set apart "one day in every week to secret prayer and fasting" for direction.[90] He also kept a diary of his experiences during this period, some of which Fuller later inserted verbatim into his *Memoirs* of Pearce and which admirably displays what Fuller described as his friend's "singular submissiveness to the will of God."[91]

During one of these days of prayer, fasting and seeking God's face—the last day of October—Pearce recorded how God met with him in a remarkable way. Pearce had begun the day with "solemn prayer for the assistance of the Holy Spirit" so that he might "enjoy the spirit and power of prayer," have his "personal religion improved," and his "public steps directed." He proceeded to read a portion of the life of the American missionary David Brainerd (1718–1747) by Jonathan Edwards (1703–1758), a book that quickened the zeal of many of Pearce's generation, and to peruse 2 Corinthians 2–6. Afterward he went to prayer, but, he recorded, his heart was hard and "all was dullness," and he feared that somehow he had offended God.[92]

Suddenly, Pearce wrote, "it pleased God to smite the rock with the rod of his Spirit, and immediately the waters began to flow." Likening the frame of his heart to the rock in the desert that Moses struck with his rod in order to bring forth water from it (see Exodus 17:1–6), Pearce had found himself unable to generate any

---

89 Payne, "Samuel Pearce," 50.

90 Fuller, *Memoirs of the Rev. Samuel Pearce*, 42.

91 Fuller, *Memoirs of the Rev. Samuel Pearce*, 79. For the diary, see Fuller, *Memoirs of the Rev. Samuel Pearce*, 43–78. For some extracts from the diary, see also Haykin, "Samuel Pearce, Extracts from a Diary," 9–18.

92 Fuller, *Memoirs of the Rev. Samuel Pearce*, 72–74.

profound warmth for God and his dear cause. God, as it were, had to come by his Spirit, "touch" Pearce's heart and so quicken his affections. He was overwhelmed, he wrote, by "a heavenly glorious melting power." He saw afresh "the love of a crucified Redeemer" and "the attractions of his cross." He felt "like Mary [Madgalene] at the master's feet weeping, for tenderness of soul; like a little child, for submission to my heavenly father's will." The need to take the gospel to those who had never heard it gripped him anew "with an irresistible drawing of soul" and, in his own words, "compelled me to vow that I would, by his leave, serve him among the heathen."[93] As he wrote later in his diary:

> If ever in my life I knew anything of the influences of the Holy Spirit, I did at this time. I was swallowed up in God. Hunger, fulness, cold, heat, friends and enemies, all seemed nothing before God. I was in a new world. All was delightful; for Christ was all, and in all. Many times I concluded prayer, but when rising from my knees, communion with God was so desirable, that I was sweetly drawn to it again and again, till my animal[94] strength was almost exhausted.[95]

The decision of the Society as to Pearce's status was ultimately a negative one. When the executive committee of the Society met at Roade, Northamptonshire, on November 12, it was of the opinion that Pearce could best serve the cause of missions at home in England. Pearce's response to this decision is best seen in extracts from two letters. The first, written to his wife Sarah the day after he received the decision, stated: "I am disappointed, but not dismayed. I ever wish to make my Saviour's will my own."[96] The second, sent

93 Fuller, *Memoirs of the Rev. Samuel Pearce*, 74–75.
94 i.e. physical.
95 Fuller, *Memoirs of the Rev. Samuel Pearce*, 75.
96 Fuller, *Memoirs of the Rev. Samuel Pearce*, 52. See pages 121–122.

to William Carey over four months later, contains a similar desire
to submit to the perfectly good and sovereign will of God.

> Instead of a letter, you perhaps expected to have seen the
> writer; and had the will of God been so, he would by this
> time have been on his way to Mudnabatty: but it is not
> in man that walketh to direct his steps. Full of hope and
> expectation as I was, when I wrote you last, that I should
> be honoured with a mission to the poor heathen, and be
> an instrument of establishing the empire of my dear Lord
> in India, I must submit now to stand still, and see the salva-
> tion of God.[97]

Pearce then told Carey some of the details of the November meeting at which the Society executive had made their decision regarding his going overseas.

> I shall ever love my dear brethren the more for the tender-
> ness with which they treated me, and the solemn prayer
> they repeatedly put up to God for me. At last, I withdrew
> for them to decide, and whilst I was apart from them, and
> engaged in prayer for divine direction, I felt all anxiety
> forsake me, and an entire resignation of will to the will of
> God, be it what it would, together with a satisfaction that
> so much praying breath would not be lost; but that he
> who hath promised to be found of all that seek him, would
> assuredly direct the hearts of my brethren to that which
> was most pleasing to himself, and most suitable to the in-
> terests of his kingdom in the world. Between two and

---

97 Letter to William Carey, March 27, 1795 (*Missionary Correspondence: containing
Extracts of Letters from the late Mr. Samuel Pearce, to the Missionaries in India, Between
the Years 1794 and 1798; and from Mr. John Thomas, from 1798 to 1800* [London: T.
Gardiner and Son, 1814], 26).

three hours were they deliberating after which time a paper was put into my hands, of which the following is a copy.

> The brethren at this meeting are fully satisfied of the fitness of brother P[earce]'s qualifications, and greatly approve of the disinterestedness of his motives and the ardour of his mind. But another Missionary not having been requested, and not being in our view immediately necessary, and brother P[earce] occupying already a post very important to the prosperity of the Mission itself, we are unanimously of opinion that at present, however, he should continue in the situation which he now occupies.[98]

In response to this decision, which dashed some of Pearce's deepest longings, he was, he said, "enabled cheerfully to reply, 'The will of the Lord be done;' and receiving this answer as the voice of God, I have, for the most part, been easy since, though not without occasional pantings of spirit after the publishing of the gospel to the Pagans."[99]

From the vantage-point of the highly individualistic spirit of twenty-first century Western Christianity, Pearce's friends seem to have been quite wrong in refusing to send him to India. If, during his month of fasting and prayer, he had felt he knew God's will for his life, was not the Baptist Missionary Society executive wrong in the decision they made? And should not Pearce have persisted in pressing his case for going?[100] While these questions may seem natural ones to ask given the cultural matrix of contemporary

---

98 Letter to William Carey, March 27, 1795 (*Missionary Correspondence*, 30–31). For more of this letter, see pages 125–129.

99 Letter to William Carey, March 27, 1795 (*Missionary Correspondence*, 31).

100 These were actual questions posed to me after I gave a lecture entitled "The Spirituality of Samuel Pearce" at Toronto Baptist Seminary and Bible College on November 28, 1998.

Western Christianity, Pearce knew himself to be part of a team and he was more interested in the triumph of that team's strategy than the fulfilment of his own personal desires.[101]

## *"Surely Irish Zion demands our prayers"*

Pearce's passion for the lost found outlet in other ways. In July 1795, he received an invitation from the General Evangelical Society in Dublin to come over to Dublin and preach at a number of venues. He was not able to go until the following year, when he left Birmingham at 8 A.M. on May 31. After travelling through Wales and taking passage on a ship from Holyhead, he landed in Dublin on Saturday afternoon, June 4.[102]

While in Dublin, Pearce stayed with a Presbyterian elder by the name of Hutton who was a member of a congregation pastored by a Dr. McDowell.[103] Pearce preached for this congregation on a number of occasions, as well as for other congregations in the city, including the Baptists. Calvinistic Baptist witness in Dublin went back to the Cromwellian period of 1653 when, through the ministry of Thomas Patient (d.1666), the first Calvinistic Baptist meeting-house was built in Swift's Alley.[104] The church grew rapidly at first, and, by 1725, this church had between 150 and 200 members.[105] A new meeting-house was put up in the 1730s.

---

101  See Ralph D. Winter, "William Carey's Major Novelty" in J.T.K. Daniel and R.E. Hedlund, eds., *Carey's Obligation and India's Renaissance* (Serampore, West Bengal: Council of Serampore College, 1993), 136–137.

102  Samuel Pearce, Letter to Sarah Pearce, June 4, 1796 (Samuel Pearce Mss.).

103  Samuel Pearce, Letter to Sarah Pearce, June 4, 1796 (Samuel Pearce Mss.).

104  B.R. White, "Thomas Patient in England and Ireland," *Irish Baptist Historical Society Journal*, 2 (1969–1970): 41. See also Robert Dunlop, "Dublin Baptists from 1650 Onwards," *Irish Baptist Historical Society Journal*, 21 (1988–1989): 6–7.

105  Joshua Thompson, "Baptists in Ireland 1792–1922: A Dimension of Protestant Dissent" (Unpublished D. Phil. Thesis, Regent's Park College, University of Oxford, 1988), 9.

By the time that Pearce came to Ireland in 1796, though, membership had declined to roughly forty members. Pearce's impressions of the congregation were not too positive. In a letter he wrote to William Carey in August 1796, the month after his return to England, he told the missionary:

> There were 10 Baptist societies in Ireland.—They are now reduced to 6 & bid fair soon to be perfectly extinct.
>
> When I came to Dublin they had no meeting of any kind for religious purposes.... Indeed they were so dead to piety that, tho' of their own denomination, I saw & knew less of them than of every other professors in the place.[106]

This situation does not appear to have dampened Pearce's zeal in preaching. A Dublin deacon by the name of Howard wrote to John Rippon:"We have had a jubilee for some weeks.That blessed man of God, Mr. Pearce, has preached among us with great sweetness, and with much power."[107] Pearce was also delighted to find a number of young men training for the Anglican ministry at Trinity College, who, as Pearce put it, were "vigorously exerting themselves in various places, on behalf of evangelical piety."Time spent in their company discussing the Christian life and praying were some of the happiest memories Pearce took away from his time in Ireland.[108] Pearce's passionate concern for the advance of the gospel in Ireland is well caught in a sentence from one of his letters to his wife Sarah. "Surely," he wrote to her on June 24, "*Irish* Zion demands our prayers."[109]

---

106 Letter to William Carey, August, 1796 (Samuel Pearce Carey Collection—Pearce Family Letters).

107 John Rippon,"A short account of The General Evangelical Society in Dublin, and of the state of Religion in that vicinity," *Baptist Annual Register*, 2:408.

108 Samuel Pearce, Letter to John Rippon, August, 1796 (*Baptist Annual Register*, 2:406).

109 Letter to Sarah Pearce, June 24, 1796 (Samuel Pearce Mss.). For a letter that

## *"Who can tell what God might do!"*

In the three remaining years of Pearce's earthly life, he expended much of his energy in raising support for the cause of foreign missions. As he informed Carey in the fall of 1797:

> I can hardly refrain from repeating what I have so often told you before, that I long to meet you on earth and to join you in your labours of love among the poor dear heathens. Yes, would my Lord bid me so, I should with transport obey the summons and take a joyful farewell of the land that bare me, though it were for ever. But I must confess that the path of duty appears to me clearer than before to be at home, at least for the present. Not that I think my connexions in England a sufficient argument, but that I am somewhat necessary to the Mission itself, and shall be as long as money is wanted and our number of active friends does not increase. Brother Fuller and myself have the whole of the collecting business on our hands, and though there are many others about us who exceed me in grace and gifts, yet their other engagements forbid or their peculiar turn of mind disqualifies them for that kind of service. I wish, however, to be thankful if our dear Lord will but employ me as a foot in the body. I consider myself as united to the hands and eyes, and mouth, and heart, and all; and when the body rejoices, I have my share of gladness with the other members.[110]

---

Pearce wrote to a young man that he met on this trip to Ireland, see pages 153–155.
110  Letter to William Carey, September 8, 1797 (*Missionary Correspondence*, 53–54).

One of the meetings at which Pearce preached was the one that saw William Ward (1769–1823)—later to be one of the most invaluable of Carey's co-workers in India—accepted as a missionary with the Baptist Missionary Society. Those attending the meeting, which took place at Kettering on October 16, 1798, were deeply stirred by Pearce's passion and concern for the advance of the gospel. He preached "like an Apostle," Fuller later wrote to Carey. And when Ward wrote to Carey, he told his future colleague that Pearce "set the whole meeting in a flame. Had missionaries been needed, we might have had a cargo immediately."[111]

Returning back to Birmingham from this meeting, Pearce was caught in a heavy downpour of rain, drenched to the skin, and subsequently developed a severe chill. Neglecting to rest and foolishly thinking what he called "pulpit sweats" would effect a cure, he continued a rigorous schedule of preaching at Cannon Street as well as in outlying villages around Birmingham. His lungs became so inflamed that Pearce had to ask William Ward to supply the Cannon Street pulpit. As Pearce wrote Ward in a letter:

> Do you want time? You shall have it here. Do you want books? You shall have them here. Do you want a friend? Be assured, the hand, that moves this pen, belongs to a heart warmly attached to you. If you love me—come and help me. Come and secure the hearts and prayers of the hundreds of Birmingham Christians, who only want to know you, to love you too.[112]

---

111 Andrew Fuller, Letter to William Carey, April 18, 1799 (Letters of Andrew Fuller, Typescript transcript, Angus Library, Regent's Park College, University of Oxford); William Ward, Letter to William Carey, October 1798 (cited S. Pearce Carey, *William Carey*, ed. Peter Masters [London: Wakeman Trust, 1993], 172). Fuller noted that Pearce's sermon was "full of a holy unction" and "seemed to breathe an apostolical ardor" (Fuller, *Memoirs of the Rev. Samuel Pearce*, 127).

112 Cited Samuel Stennett, *Memoirs of the Life of the Rev. William Ward* (2nd ed.; London: J. Haddon, 1825), 55–56. This Samuel Stennett is not to be confused with

Pearce and Ward appear to have thought that this arrangement would be for only a few weeks. As it was, Ward ended up staying for three months, from mid-December 1798 to the beginning of March 1799.[113] The two men developed a deep friendship, as Ward later told Pearce, "your name, your virtues are engraven on my heart in indelible characters."[114]

Pearce preached his last sermon at Cannon Street on December 2, 1798,[115] and soon found that he could not converse for more than a few minutes without losing his breath. Yet still he was thinking of the salvation of the lost. He wrote what E.A. Payne termed "an eloquent tract" to be given to the Lascars, that is, Indian or Southeast-Asian sailors, who were employed on board British naval vessels or who worked in the British ports, some ten thousand or so of them.[116] Also, writing to Carey around this time, he told him of a plan to take the gospel to France that he had been mulling over in his mind. At that time, Great Britain and France were locked in a titanic war, the Napoleonic War, which would last into the middle of the second decade of the next century. This war was the final and climactic

---

the well-known London Baptist pastor, Dr. Samuel Stennett (1727–1795). This Stennett was a friend of William Ward and pastored in Dublin, Ireland, for a period of time. See A. Christopher Smith, "William Ward, Radical Reform, and Missions in the 1790s," *American Baptist Quarterly*, 10, No.3 (September 1991): 240, n.1.

113 Stennett, *Life of the Rev. William Ward*, 55–56. On Ward, see the just-cited *Life of the Rev. William Ward* and A. Christopher Smith, "William Ward, Radical Reform, and Missions," 218–244; *idem*, "The Legacy of William Ward and Joshua and Hannah Marshman," *International Bulletin of Missionary Research*, 23, No.3 (July 1999): 120–129; *idem*, "William Ward (1769–1823)" in Haykin, ed., *British Particular Baptists*, II, 254–271; E.I. Carlyle, "William Ward," revised Brian Stanley in *Oxford Dictionary of National Biography*, eds. H.C.G. Matthew and Brian Harrison (Oxford: Oxford University Press, 2004), 57:360–361.

114 Letter from William Ward, May 13, 1799, cited "Biographical Notices: The Rev. Samuel Pearce" in John Taylor, *Biographies. Northamptonshire* (Northampton: Taylor & Son, 1901), 12.

115 Fuller, *Memoirs of the Rev. Samuel Pearce*, 135. The sermon was on Daniel 10:19.

116 *First Generation*, 50.

episode in a struggle that had dominated the eighteenth century. Not surprisingly, there was little love lost between the British and the French. Samuel Carter Hall (1800–1889), a Victorian literary figure, for example, recalled that one of his earliest memories as a young boy was his father putting him on his knee and telling him, "Be a good boy, love your mother, and hate the French"![117]

But Pearce was gripped by a far different passion than those that gripped many in Britain and France—his was the priority of the kingdom of Christ. In one of the last sermons that he ever preached, on a day of public thanksgiving for the victory of Horatio Nelson (1758–1805) over the French fleet at the Battle of the Nile (1798) and the defeat of a French invasion of Ireland that fall, Pearce pointedly said:

> Should any one expect that I shall introduce the *destruction* of our foes, by the late victories gained off the coasts of Egypt and Ireland, as the object of pleasure and gratitude, he will be disappointed. The man who can take pleasure at the destruction of his fellow men, is a cannibal at heart;... but to the heart of him who calls himself a disciple of the merciful Jesus, let such pleasure be an everlasting stranger. Since in that sacred volume, which I revere as the fair gift of heaven to man, I am taught, that "of one blood God hath made all nations," [Acts 17:26] it is impossible for me not to regard every man as my brother, and to consider, that national differences ought not to excite personal animosities.[118]

---

117 *Retrospect of a Long Life: from 1815 to 1883* (New York: D. Appleton and Co., 1883), 45.

118 *Motives to Gratitude*, 18–19. It is noteworthy that the French Reformer John Calvin (1509–1564) could also say, "Let a Moor or a Barbarian come among us, and yet inasmuch as he is a man, he brings with him a looking glass wherein we may see that he is our brother and neighbor." (*Sermons of M. Iohn Caluine vpon the Epistle*

A few months later—when he was desperately ill—he wrote a letter to Carey telling him of his plans for a missionary journey to France. "I have been endeavouring for some years," he told Carey, "to get five of our Ministers to agree that they will apply themselves to the French language." Then, Pearce wrote "we"—he was obviously intending to be one of the five—"might spend two months annually in that Country, and at least satisfy ourselves that Christianity was not lost in France for want of a fair experiment in its favour: and who can tell what God might do!"[119]

God would use British evangelicals, notably Pearce's Baptist contemporary Robert Haldane (1764–1842), to take the gospel to francophones on the Continent when peace eventually came, but Pearce's anointed preaching would play no part in that great work. Yet his ardent prayers on behalf of the French could not have been without some effect. As Pearce had noted in 1794, "praying breath" is never lost.

## The "religion for a dying sinner"

By the spring of 1799 Pearce was desperately ill with pulmonary tuberculosis. Leaving his wife and family—he and Sarah had five children by this time—he went to Devon from April to July in the hope that rest there might effect a cure. When Ward and the other Baptist missionaries on their way to India were passing Plymouth in *The Criterion* on June 1, Ward prayed just this: "Oh! If it be possible—spare—spare—Oh spare his most precious life."[120]

Being away from his wife and children, though, only aggravated Pearce's suffering. Writing to Sarah—"the dear object of my

---

of *Saincte Paule to the Galathians*, trans. Arthur Golding [London, 1574], 331 (from Calvin's sermon on Galatians 6:9–11), spelling modernized).

119 Cited Carey, *Samuel Pearce*, 189.

120 "Diary of William Ward," copied Ethel M. Payne (IN/17, Baptist Missionary Archives, Angus Library, Regent's Park College, University of Oxford).

tenderest, my warmest love"—from Plymouth, he requested her to "write me as soon as you receive this" and signed it "ever, ever, ever, wholly yours." Three weeks later when he wrote, he sent Sarah "a thousand & 10 thousand thousand embraces," and then poignantly added, "may the Lord hear our daily prayers for each other!"[121]

Sarah and the children had gone to stay with her family in Alcester, twenty miles or so from Birmingham. But by mid-May Sarah could no longer bear being absent from her beloved. Leaving their children with Birmingham friends, she headed south in mid–May, where she stayed with her husband until the couple slowly made their way home to Birmingham in mid-July.[122] By this time Samuel's voice was so far gone that he could not even whisper without pain in his lungs. His suffering, though, seemed to act like a refiner's fire to draw him closer to Christ. Not long before his death, he said:

> Blessed be his dear name, who shed his blood for me. He helps me to rejoice at times with "joy unspeakable" [1 Peter 1:8]. Now I see the value of the religion of the cross. It is a religion for a dying sinner. It is all the most guilty and the most wretched can desire. Yes, I taste its sweetness, and enjoy its fulness, with all the gloom of a dying-bed before me; and far rather would I be the poor emaciated and emaciating creature that I am, than be an emperor with every earthly good about him—but without a God.[123]

A couple of years earlier, when he was preaching an expository series of sermons on Hebrews, Pearce had declared, with regard to

---

121 Letters to Sarah Pearce, April 20, 1799 and May 3, 1799 (Samuel Pearce Mss.).

122 Ernest A. Payne, "Some Samuel Pearce Documents," *The Baptist Quarterly*, 18 (1959–1960): 31.

123 Fuller, *Memoirs of the Rev. Samuel Pearce*, 176–177. For the rest of this letter, see pages 197–199.

Hebrews 11:13–16, that part of "the blessedness of true religion" was that it was a faith that enabled one to die well.[124] In the summer and early autumn of 1799, Pearce was given a profound, experimental knowledge of this truth. Some of his final words were for Sarah: "I trust our separation will not be forever…we shall meet again."[125]

He fell asleep in Christ on Thursday, October 10, 1799, and was buried the following week beneath the family pew in the Cannon Street church building. When the interior of the church was changed in later years, Pearce's grave was at the foot of the stairs leading up to the pulpit.[126] William Ward, who had been profoundly influenced by Pearce's zeal and spirituality, well summed up his character when he wrote not long before the latter's death:

> Oh! how does personal religion shine in Brother Pearce! What a soul! What a death in his soul to the world! What ardour for the glory of God! What a diffusive benevolence towards all, especially towards all who love Christ and show it by their devotion to his will! Instead of being all froth and fume, you see in him a mind wholly given up to God; a sacred lustre shines in his whole conversation; always tranquil, always cheerful, always bearing about this truth, "It is my meat and drink to do the will of my heavenly Father" [cf. John 4:34]. It is impossible to doubt the truth of experimental religion, if you are acquainted with Pearce.[127]

---

124 Sermon on Hebrews 11:13–16 in "70 sermons on the Hebrews (68) and John (2)" (Samuel Pearce Mss.). In his sermon on Hebrews 13:4, Pearce mentioned that he had been at the Baptist cause in Birmingham for "more than 7 years."

125 "The dying words of dear Brr Pearce to his wife" (Samuel Pearce Mss.).

126 Carey, *Samuel Pearce*, 215; Hale, *Cannon Street Baptist Church*, 11–12.

127 William Ward, Letter, December 31, 1798 (Stennett, *Life of the Rev. William Ward*, 58).

As Ward mentioned in another context: "I have seen more of God in him than in any other person I ever knew."[128] And when Fuller heard of Pearce's death in Scotland, he wrote to Sarah Pearce on October 19: "Try, while your mind is warm, to draw his character. Memoirs of his life must be published: he is another Brainerd."[129]

At the heart of Pearce's spirituality, both lived and taught, was the theological conviction that, as he once put it, "real religion consists in supreme love to God and disinterested [i.e. impartial] love to man."[130] Measured by this standard there seems little doubt about the reality of Pearce's Christian faith and spirituality, and also little question of the challenge it poses to Christians at the beginning of the twenty-first century.

---

128 William Ward, Letter, January 5, 1799 (Fuller, *Memoirs of the Rev. Samuel Pearce*, 138–139).

129 Cited Carey, *Samuel Pearce*, 216.

130 *Doctrine of Salvation by Free Grace Alone*, 7.

*Cannon Street Baptist Church, Birmingham*

# Chronology[1]

### July 20, 1766
Born in Plymouth

### 1766-1774
At his grandfather's home in Tamerton Foliot

### 1774-1780
At school in Plymouth

### 1780-1786
Apprentice to his father, a silversmith

### 1782
July—Conversion under the preaching of Isaiah Birt

### 1783
July 20—Baptism and becomes a member of the
Plymouth Baptist congregation

### 1786-1789
Studying at Bristol Baptist Academy

### 1789-1790
On probation at Cannon Street Baptist Church, Birmingham

### 1790
August—Ordination at Cannon Street

---

1  Based on S. Pearce Carey, *Samuel Pearce M.A., The Baptist Brainerd* (3rd ed.;
London: Carey Press, [c.1922]), 228.

## 1791
February 2—Marriage to Sarah Hopkins of Alcester

## 1791
May—First meets William Carey on the day
of Carey's ordination at Leicester

## 1792
May 4—Birth of daughter, Louisa (d.1809)
October 2—Attends the founding of the Baptist Missionary
Society (BMS) in Kettering
October 6—Forms the first BMS Auxiliary at Cannon Street
October 31—Added to the BMS Executive

## 1794
January 14—Birth of son, William Hopkins (d.1840)
May 7–8—Preaching at Guilsborough
Autumn—Praying about being a missionary in India
November 12—Meets with the BMS executive and
is turned down for India

## 1795
July 19—Birth of daughter Anna (d.1832), who
married Jonathan Carey[2]

## 1796
May-July—Preaching in Ireland

## 1797
June 8—Birth of son, Howard

---

2 Anna's birth was not registered by Samuel Pearce until 1797, at which time
he also registered his son Howard. See RG 4/2972 Cannon Street Chapel, Birmingham: Births registered 1786–1804 (The National Archives, Kew, Richmond, Surrey).

## 1798
October—Beginning of final illness
December 2—Last sermon at Cannon Street

## 1799
January—Birth of son, Samuel (d.1800)
October 10—Death of Samuel Pearce

## 1804
May 25—Death of Sarah Pearce

# Samuel Pearce

## Selections
## from his letters
## and writings

# 1

## To Isaiah Birt [1]

*Plymouth, October 27, 1782*

My very dear Mr. Birt,

Was I to make the least delay in answering your very affectionate letter, I should deem myself culpable of the greatest ingratitude to its author. Its contents so fully manifest the regard you have for me, that I am constrained to acknowledge myself under the highest obligations to you. I wish I could express it better.

You almost commence your kind letter with mentioning, that my tears at parting with you demanded your fervent prayers. But do, my dear Sir, consider, that separating from an earthly parent, the author of animal life, must, where a filial affection subsists, be an

---

1 From "Original Letter from Mr. Pearce to Mr. Birt," *The Evangelical Magazine*, 15 (1807): 111–113. Isaiah Birt pastored at Plymouth and later at Cannon Street in Birmingham from 1815 to 1827. For the life of Birt, see the account by his son: John Birt, "Memoir of the Late Rev. Isaiah Birt," *The Baptist Magazine*, 30 (1838): 54–59, 107–116, 197–203. See also Roger Hayden, *Continuity and Change: Evangelical Calvinism among Eighteenth-Century Baptist Ministers Trained at the Bristol Baptist Academy, 1690–1791* (Milton under Wychwood, Chipping Norton, Oxfordshire: Nigel Lynn Publishing, 2006), 225.

affectionate scene. How much more moving then must it be to part with a father in Christ Jesus! To part with one whom the Almighty had made the happy means of raising from a state of death in trespasses and sins, to that of life in a dear dying Redeemer!

O, Sir! Such it was when you and I parted; such was the case when I parted with my ever dear Mr. Birt. Did this require your fervent prayers? Has this caused you to remember me when prostrate at a footstool of mercy? Let me beseech you, my dear Sir, still to continue it; and whenever you bow the suppliant knee at a throne of grace, not to fail beseeching the Author of mercy to extend his mercy to an object so unworthy as myself. O! beg of him that, since he has begun a good work in me, he would carry it on.[2] As he has enabled me to put my hand to the gospel-plough, may I never look back; but may he grant me grace and strength to hold on, and hold out to the end; to conquer every foe, to be continually pressing forward toward the mark and prize of my high calling in Christ Jesus;[3] and, in the end, to come off more than conqueror through him,[4] who, I trust, has loved me and given himself for me.[5] Oh beg of him that he will ever keep me from possessing a lukewarm, a Laodicean spirit![6] May my affections to the crucified Saviour be continually on a flame.

I am "prone to wander"; yes, I feel it, "prone to leave the God I love."[7] O that my affections may be more and more united to him! My dear Sir, pray for me, and you will do your best. Use your

2  See Philippians 1:6.
3  See Philippians 3:14.
4  See Romans 8:37.
5  See Galatians 2:20.
6  An allusion to Revelation 3:16.
7  A quotation from the third stanza of the hymn of Robert Robinson (1735–1790), "Come, Thou Fount of every blessing." For a study of this hymn, see Michael A.G. Haykin, "'Come, Thou Fount of Every Blessing': Robert Robinson's Hymnic Celebration of Sovereign Grace" in Steve West, ed., *Ministry of Grace: Essays in Honor of John G. Reisinger* (Frederick, Maryland: New Covenant Media, 2007), 31–43.

interest at a throne of grace on my behalf; and as God has promised to be a God hearing and answering prayer,[8] and as he is willing and able to perform all his promise, I doubt not but it will meet with a reception, and perhaps with a gracious answer too. O, Sir! Let me once more entreat you never to forget me whilst offering up prayers to your God. Religion, you may well say, is worthy the choice of all: it makes a beggar superior to a king. Whilst destitute of it, a king is inferior to a beggar.... What can equal the felicity, the enjoyments of a Christian? Nothing, surely, on this transitory globe! Nothing this world calls good or great can be put in competition with it—with the joyous feeling of him, who has the unspeakable happiness of experiencing himself interested in a dear Redeemer. He feels that

> Which nothing earthly gives, or can destroy,
> The soul's calm sunshine and the heartfelt joy.[9]

Yes, the happiness he feels is beyond all conception, beyond all the stretch of human thought. Is there aught to be compared with serving the Lord? Surely, no.

> Pleasure springs fresh for ever thence,
> Unspeakable, unknown![10]

---

8  Cf. Psalm 65:2, where God is addressed thus: "O thou that hearest prayer." In the circles in which Pearce moved, this emphasis about God was common. It is noteworthy that Jonathan Edwards, whose writings deeply influenced the circle of men around Pearce, preached a sermon entitled, "The Most High A Prayer-Hearing God," which was published in *Practical Sermons, Never Before Published* (Edinburgh: M. Gray, 1788), 67–85, and which was read by William Carey on his way to India.

9  Alexander Pope, *An Essay On Man*, Epistle IV, lines 167–168. This poem was printed in numerous editions in the eighteenth century, any one of which Pearce could have used.

10  These lines come from a hymn of Isaac Watts (1674–1748): "Father, I long, I faint to see/The place of thine abode," stanza 3, *Hymns and Spiritual Songs in Three Books*, Book 2, Hymn 68 in George Burder, compiled, *The Works of the Reverend and*

But that which adds to its reality is its permanence. It is not confined to this life only; what we have here is but a foretaste of those joys which accompany our immortal part to the bright realms of day, where we shall have joy added to joy, pleasure to pleasure, and there

> Shall drink immortal vigour in,
> With wonder and with love.[11]

Surely, no tongue can express, no heart can conceive, what God has prepared for those who love him![12]

Oh how abundantly thankful then ought those to be, whom he has called by divine grace to the knowledge of himself! What an unspeakable mercy is it, that he has called me by divine grace to the knowledge of himself! What an unspeakable mercy is it, that he has distinguished me in such a peculiar manner, as to (give me leave to use your own words) be taken into his service, adopted into his family, made an heir of God, a joint heir with Jesus Christ! What now is required of me? What am I now required to do? When I reflect on this, how short do I come in my duty! How backward am I to it! How unwilling to perform it! Even "when I would do good, evil is present with me."[13]

...I have no righteousness of my own, no merits of mine to bring; the best of my performances come infinitely short of the holy law of God. On Jesus alone then I must depend for salvation. Here I rest. Hence I draw all my hope. Jesus Christ has died, and Jesus shall

---

Learned Isaac Watts, D.D. (London: John Barfield, 1810), IV, 317.

11 These lines come from the hymn of Isaac Watts mentioned in n.10: "Father, I long, I faint to see/The place of thy abode," stanza 4, *Hymns and Spiritual Songs in Three Books*, Book 2, Hymn 68 in Burder, compiled, *Works of the Reverend and Learned Isaac Watts*, IV, 317. Pearce has added the word "shall" at the beginning of his quote to make it fit with his sentence.

12 See 1 Corinthians 2:9.

13 Romans 7:21.

not die in vain. The Redeemer's blood cleanses from all sin. Happy, thrice happy they who have washed and made their robes white in the blood of the Lamb! May it be the blessed experience of my dear friend and me!\

I thank you, Sir, for your kind admonitions. I hope the God of all grace will enable me to abide by them. Tribulations, trials, and temptations, I am sensible, are the lot of all God's children here below; but I am equally certain, that, as long as we rely upon our God, and confide in him only, he that has given us a sure word of promise, whereby he has caused us to hope, will with them all work out a way for our escape, that we may be able to hear them.[14]

And now, that it may be our joint happiness, my dear Sir, to be kept in a holy, happy fellowship with our God; that we may be often brought to Pisgah's summit and behold the promised Canaan[15]; that we may often, whilst there, anticipate the pleasures of the heavenly world; and, when we have passed the floods of Jordan, meet around the throne above, there to chant eternal lays to "Him that sitteth upon the throne, and to the Lamb forever,"[16] is, Dear Sir, the constant prayer of him who is, and wishes ever to remain,

Your affectionate friend,
Samuel Pearce.

---

14 See 1 Corinthians 10:13.
15 See Deuteronomy 34, a reference to Moses seeing the land of Canaan from Mount Pisgah.
16 Revelation 5:13.

# 2

## Samuel Pearce's
## Confession of Faith[1]

Religion of every description originates in the belief of a God, the author of our existence, the preserver of our lives, and the object of our worship.

Convinced from the varied scenes of infinite wisdom, power and goodness, which present themselves on every hand, I do believe in one self–existent, independent, almighty, omnipotent, and unchangeable Being, who is the great origin of all, who is in all, and through all, and over all, God blessed for evermore. A Being whose majesty teaches me to revere him, his goodness to love him, his faithfulness to trust him, and his universal dominion to worship and adore him.

I believe that this eternal God, for the benefit of his rational creatures in this world, hath been pleased to reveal unto them, by

---

1 From Andrew Fuller, *Memoirs of the Rev. Samuel Pearce*, ed. W.H. Pearce (London: G. Wightman, 1831), 8–13. The original is in the Bristol Baptist College Archives, Ms G96 BMS Box 14658. Footnotes indicating Scripture citations and allusions have been kept to a minimum.

different modes and in different ages, that information which was necessary for the regulation of their faith and conduct; that what remains of this revelation is contained in the Holy Scriptures, or those books usually called the Old and New Testament; that the books therein contained declare the very mind and will of God, and were written by holy men of old, under his immediate inspiration; that this revelation is so complete as to need no addition, and declares every truth necessary to be believed, and every duty God requires to be performed by man; and that its Author has been pleased to give such demonstrations of its authenticity as are wholly adequate to the satisfaction of every honest mind.

By these Scriptures, I am instructed in those important truths which respect the nature, perfections and operations of God; and, on their alone testimony, I believe that, though the essence of the Godhead is one, yet there are three who bear record in heaven, the Father, the Word and the Holy Ghost; that the Father is truly and properly God; the Son is truly and properly God; and the Holy Ghost truly and properly God; and yet there are not three Gods, but one God, in essence, power and glory; and though I confess this is a mystery, incomprehensible by mortals, yet on the testimony of Scripture, which I conceive fully and expressly to teach the doctrine of the Trinity in Unity, I submit to the authority of revelation; and, as I cannot fathom, I wish to trust.

Agreeable to Scripture information,

I believe that in the beginning God created the heavens and the earth in six days; and having designed this world for, and suited it to, the condition of a rational creature, he made man in his own image, with a mind formed for loving and obeying its Creator; but at the same time, in perfect consistency with that freedom of the will with which, for the honour and justice of divine government, he endues all his intelligent creatures.

I believe that God wisely appointed a test for the obedience of man, wonderfully suited to his nature and state, promising a continuance of felicity co-equal with a continuance of duty; but threatening death as the consequence of a violation of his law, including not only subjection of the body to mortality, but also a loss of the moral image of God, and liability to everlasting misery, as the just reward of sin.

I believe that man voluntarily and willingly, without any necessity from the purpose of God, did violate this law, and thereby expose himself to all of its penalties; and that, from the connection of the whole human race with Adam, all his posterity are so interested in his conduct as through his fate to become possessors of a corrupt nature, which, being opposed to the righteous will of God, constitutes us objects of his displeasure, and disposes us to that conduct which terminates in eternal death; or, in the language of Scripture, "Sin having entered into the world, death came by sin, so that death hath passed upon all men, for that all have sinned."[2]

I believe that, before the world began, God (foreseeing the dreadful calamities which mankind would bring upon themselves) did, of his own free and sovereign purpose and grace, choose a certain number of the human race unto everlasting salvation, making provision for this display of his mercy, in perfect harmony with the justice of his character, in the covenant of grace, by which all things appertaining to the redemption of the elect were ordered and made sure. I believe that the Son of God, the second person in the adorable Trinity, having thus engaged to effect the salvation of his people, in entire consistency with the divine perfections, did in the fullness of time (agreeably to ancient prophecies) unite himself to human nature, being miraculously conceived by the virgin of the Holy Ghost; that in that nature he obeyed, suffered and died on behalf of the elect of God, whose sins were imputed to him, and the punishment of which he bore in his own body on the tree, suffering, the just for the unjust, to bring them to God, making a plenary

---

2 See Romans 5:12.

satisfaction to almighty justice for all their transgressions, and effecting a complete righteousness, which, being imputed to them on believing, becomes the matter of their justification before God.

I believe that the sacrifice of Christ is so efficacious, and his righteousness so complete, that for the sake of his merits alone, independently of any holiness of the creature, the transgressions of believers are forgiven, they are reconciled to God, receive the adoption of sons, and become heirs of everlasting glory.

I believe that, in order to our preparation to eternal life, the work of the Holy Spirit of God in us is as necessary as the work of Christ for us; that the Holy Spirit is the author of regeneration, and all its fruits, as repentance, faith, love, hope, joy, peace, purity and meetness for heaven; that all the elect of God have been, are, or shall be made, the subjects of this efficacious grace; and that none have the least reason to conclude themselves the objects of the divine favour whose hearts are not renewed, and whose lives are not sanctified by this divine Spirit—for "without holiness no man shall see the Lord."[3]

I believe that all those who are thus renewed by the Holy Ghost in the spirit of their minds shall certainly and finally persevere in grace, and attain to everlasting glory, notwithstanding all the opposition they meet with from the world, the flesh, and the devil, being "kept by the power of God through faith unto salvation."[4]

I believe that when death puts a period to man's existence, and his body returns to the dust, his soul returns to God who gave it, then to receive an immediate consciousness of its future destiny, in which state it remains, either in certain expectation of unutterable misery, or delightful anticipation of eternal enjoyment, till the judgement day.

I believe that there will be a resurrection of the dead, both of the just and of the unjust, to which shall succeed the general judgement,

---

3   Cf. Hebrews 12:14.
4   1 Peter 1:5.

when all the human race shall be impartially judged according to the deeds done in the body, whether good or evil; that those who died in a state of impenitency and unbelief shall throughout eternity endure the most exquisite torments, as the due reward of their sins against God; but those who have been interested in the atonement of Jesus Christ, are renewed by grace, and made meet for glory, shall be introduce to everlasting honour and joy, even to God's right hand, "where there is fullness of joy, and pleasures for evermore."[5] At that period, the conduct of the Almighty, however dark and inexplicable to us now, shall be, by all God's intelligent creation, acknowledged just, both in the condemnation of the sinner and the salvation of the saint.

I believe that in order to accomplish the purposes of the grace of God, respecting the calling, sanctifying and saving of his people, Jesus Christ hath appointed a Gospel ministry, to continue in the world till the end of time, when all the elect shall be gathered in; that it is the duty of all those who are called by grace to unite in Christian communion, and publicly to assemble for the purposes of divine worship; and that a number of Christians united in one faith, and by mutual consent thus assembling together, yielding obedience to the laws of Jesus Christ, constitute a Christian church.

I believe that, in order to become a member of a visible church of Christ, it is necessary that the person be baptized, on a profession of repentance and faith, in the name of the Father, the Son and the Holy Ghost. That baptism is only Scripturally and acceptably administered by the immersion of the body in water; and that none but believers in the Christian faith have a right to this ordinance.

I believe that, for wise ends, Jesus Christ hath appointed the sacrament called the Lord's Supper (or a participation of bread and wine by his people, when assembled together) to be continued in

---

5 Psalm 16:11.

his church, both in remembrance of his vicarious sacrifice for their sins, and also to unite them more to one another in love.

I believe that a society of Christians, or a Christian church thus formed, is wholly independent of any synod, council or other ecclesiastical magistracy, and has the sole right of conducting its own affairs (as the choosing of a minister, admission or exclusion of members and the administration of the various parts of church discipline) without the interference of any man, or body of men whatever, whether civil or ecclesiastical; and that it is the duty of all the friends of Christianity to withstand every encroachment on the liberties of their conscience, or their conduct, by which the peace and good of society is not injured, that hereby they may prove themselves the true disciples of him who hath said, "my kingdom is not of this world."[6]

These are the opinions which, from what I deem sufficient evidence, I profess cordially to embrace. These are the sentiments I have invariably endeavoured to defend, since providence led me to this town. These truths I think it my honour to avow before so respectable an assembly this day; and these I mean, through divine assistance, to maintain, defend, and enforce, in my future ministry, unless I should find superior evidence than hitherto I have found in favour of different opinions.

---

6 John 18:36.

# 3

# *[To William Summers ?]*[1]

## *September 1, 1790*

Genuine friendships are seldom formed in haste; but there is no

---

1 From "Extracts from Mr. Pearce's Letters," *The Baptist Magazine*, 1 (1809): 54–55. The recipient of this letter, who actually submitted this letter and another by Pearce to himself for publication in *The Baptist Magazine*, identifies himself by the pen-name "Epenetus," taken from the brother mentioned in Romans 16:5. It was common in this period for some Baptist authors to use Greek and Latin pen-names. For example, Andrew Fuller often used the pen-name of Gaius when writing occasional pieces for periodicals. This recipient does mention in his prefatory remarks to this letter that it was "addressed to an intimate and highly respected friend of Mr. Pearce, whose name frequently occurs in the *Memoirs*" ("Extracts from Mr. Pearce's Letters," 54). There are only three men who could possibly be the recipient given this description. Since Andrew Fuller and John Ryland are actually mentioned in the body of this letter, it cannot be either of them. This leaves then Pearce's London friend William Summers, who was among the closest of his friends. Summers is explicitly mentioned a number of times in Fuller, *Memoirs of the Rev. Samuel Pearce*. According to Fuller, Pearce opened his heart to Summers "without reserve" (*Memoirs of the Rev. Samuel Pearce*, 26).

Summers was an ironmonger—he is described as a "tinman" in *The Universal British Dictionary* (London, 1790), 303)—who lived first at 98 New Bond Street, general rule without some exceptions.[2] The uniform feelings of my heart since I parted with you tell me so. Accept, my dear friend, the avowal of my sincere attachment; accept my acknowledgements for the repeated acts of kindness which have so lately distinguished your conduct towards me. May a gracious providence make those requitals to which I am inadequate; that as the pleasures of social intercourse with others have been pursued by you, yourself may never mourn the absence of that refined bliss which the communion of kindred minds inspires.

You were informed before you left Warwickshire of the day on which the sacred union was expected to take place between me and the dear people in Cannon Street, namely, Aug. 18.[3] The day arrived, and we were publicly joined in gospel bonds.[4] Rev. Dr. Evans delivered a very faithful and affectionate charge from 2 Corinthians 4:1–2. Rev. Rob. Hall, Sen. addressed the people in a manner equally suitable and affectionate from Deuteronomy 1:38.[5] Mr.

---

London, and then moved to 105 Bond Street ("Appendix. Subscriptions, Collections, and Donations" in *Periodical Accounts relative to the Baptist Missionary Society* [London: W. Button, 1810], IV, 307 and 484). As now, Bond Street was a very prestigious area of London. His final years were spent at West End House, Wickwar, Gloucestershire ("Obituary: Memoir of the Late Stephen Prust, Esq., Bristol," *The Evangelical Magazine and Missionary Chronicle*, n.s., 29 [1851]: 276). For further discussion of his friendship with Pearce, see S. Pearce Carey, *Samuel Pearce, M.A., The Baptist Brainerd* (3rd ed.; London: Carey Press, n.d.), 111–112. See also Samuel Pearce, Letter to William Summers, July 12, 1798, in Timothy Whelan, transcribed and ed., *Baptist Autographs in the John Rylands University Library of Manchester, 1741–1845* (Macon, Georgia: Mercer University Press, 2009), 88–89.

2  Compare Pearce's remarks to Samuel Etheridge: "in our path thro life, tho we meet with so many travelers, & we hope with many who are going to Zion with their faces thitherward; yet, it is not often that we meet with men, whose openness of mind, steadiness of attachment, & spirituality of temper, invite our friendship with...force & sweetness" (Letter to Samuel Etheridge, April 20, 1796 [Whelan, transcribed and ed., *Baptist Autographs*, 83]).

3  See page 8.

4  On Caleb Evans, see pages 5–6.

5  Robert Hall, Sr. (1728–1791) was the pastor of a small Baptist cause in Arnesby, Leicestershire, from 1753 till his death. Hall's *Help to Zion's Travellers* (1781) was seen

*[To William Summers?]*

Fuller offered the ordination prayer on behalf of the pastor, and Mr. Ryland for five deacons who were at the same time set apart to their office.[6]

---

as a very important reply to late eighteenth-century Hyper-Calvinism, which was then regnant in far too many Calvinistic Baptist quarters. Hall argued that the preaching of the gospel should not be restricted in any way, but that men and women everywhere and in every condition need to be exhorted to repent and believe on Christ for salvation. It is hardly surprising that William Carey, who frequently walked the thirty miles from Olney to Arnesby to hear Hall preach, would later declare of his first encounter with this book: "I do not remember ever to have read any book with such raptures" (cited Raymond Brown, *The English Baptists of the Eighteenth Century* [London: The Baptist Historical Society, 1986], 116). And Hall's own son, Robert Hall, Jr., in a preface which he wrote for a later edition of *Help to Zion's Travellers* in 1814, declared: "To this treatise, and to another on a similar subject by my excellent and judicious friend Mr. Fuller, the dissenters in general, and the Baptists in particular, are under great obligation for emancipating them from the fetters of prejudice, and giving free scope to the publication of the gospel." ("Preface" to *Help to Zion's Travellers* in *The Works of the Rev. Robert Hall, A.M.*, eds. Olinthus Gregory and Joseph Belcher [New York: Harper & Brothers, 1854], II, 452). A contemporary edition of Hall's book is now available: Robert Hall, *Help to Zion's Travellers,* Nathan Finn, ed. (Mountain Home: BorderStone Press, 2011). The work of Andrew Fuller to which the younger Hall was referring in the above quote was Fuller's *The Gospel Worthy of All Acceptation*, which was first published in 1785.

For further reading on Hall, see John Rippon, ed., *The Baptist Annual Register* (London, 1790–1793), 1:226–241; Joseph Ivimey, *A History of the English Baptists* (London: Isaac Taylor Hinton and Holdsworth & Ball, 1830), IV, 603–609; William Cathcart, ed. *The Baptist Encyclopaedia* (Philadelphia: Louis H. Everts, 1883), 487–488; Robert Hall Warren, *The Hall Family* (Bristol: J.W. Arrowsmith, 1910), 5–27; Graham Hughes, "Robert Hall of Arnesby: 1728–1791," *The Baptist Quarterly*, 10 (1940–1941): 444–447; Michael A.G. Haykin, "Robert Hall, Sr. (1728–1791)" in Michael A.G. Haykin, ed., *The British Particular Baptists 1638–1910* (Springfield, Missouri: Particular Baptist Press, 1998), I, 203–211.

6  John Ryland, Jr. was one of Pearce's closest friends and a central figure in the formation of the Baptist Missionary Society. With Pearce, he wholly shared Andrew Fuller's evangelical Calvinism. Ryland pastored with his father, John C. Ryland (1723–1792) in Northampton for a number of years before moving to Bristol in 1793, where, until his death in 1825, he was the pastor of Broadmead Church and the principal of Bristol Baptist Academy. For his life and ministry, see especially "Memoir of the Late Rev. John Ryland, D.D.," *The Baptist Magazine*, 18 (1826): 1–9; J.E. Ryland, "Memoir" in *Pastoral Memorials: Selected from the Manuscripts of the Late*

Nearly thirty ministers were present. The service was admirably conducted: it was a very solemn, interesting and affecting season to many. We all enjoyed it, because, I trust, we enjoyed God in it. Myself and others much wished for the presence of our good friend: it would have added to our joy, and we hoped it would have been no small addition to his own. But we are always best where providence directs us: by and by we hope to be all present with the Saviour. If grace brings us there at last, we shall not regret the momentary departures from one another which we realize below. This thought often supports me under many transient removals. It was attended with no small degree of pain that I was called to leave my beloved charge almost as soon as I became their pastor (the Monday after) and that for six Sabbaths; but it was a prior engagement and unavoidable.[7] May the chief Shepherd take care of them in my absence, and keep them holy, humble, spiritual, affectionate, prayerful and thankful.

---

*Revd. John Ryland, D.D.* (London: B.J. Holdsworth, 1826), I, 1–56; L.G. Champion, "The Letters of John Newton to John Ryland," *The Baptist Quarterly*, 27 (1977–1978): 157–163; *idem*, "The Theology of John Ryland: Its Sources and Influences," *The Baptist Quarterly*, 28 (1979–1980): 17–29; Grant Gordon, ed., *Wise Counsel: John Newton's Letters to John Ryland, Jr.* (Edinburgh/Carlisle, Pennsylvania: The Banner of Truth Trust, 2009).

Three of the elements mentioned in this outline that Pearce gives of his ordination service—the charge to the pastor, the charge to the church and the ordination prayer—were typically found in Baptist ordinations during this era. For another account of this ordination, see "Ordinations in 1790, 1791, 1792: Mr. Samuel Pearce" in Rippon, ed., *Baptist Annual Register*, 1:517. On Calvinistic Baptist ordinations in general in this era, see Nigel David Wheeler, "Eminent Spirituality and Eminent Usefulness: Andrew Fuller's (1754–1815) Pastoral Theology in His Ordination Sermons" (Unpublished Ph.D. thesis, University of Pretoria, 2009), 76–117.

7   Pearce is referring to one of the conditions of his becoming pastor of the Cannon Street congregation, namely, that he be given six weeks annually to visit his father in Plymouth. See page 8.

# 4

## *To Sarah Hopkins*[1]

*Birmingham, [Friday], December 24, 1790*

My dear Sarah,

Were I averse to writing, as children are to haunted houses or ghostly church yards at midnight, one of your dear epistles could not fail of conquering the antipathy and transforming it into desire. The moment I peruse a line from my Sarah, I am inspired at the propensity which never leaves me, till I have thrown open my whole heart, and returned a copy of it to the dear being who long since compelled it to a *voluntary surrender*, and whose claims have never since been disputed.

...I have been so in the habit of being indulged with a fresh testimony of your friendship on *Thursdays*, that I begin to feel my philosophy unable to withstand the shock of disappointment, if that day...you are silent. How impatiently did I walk, & sit, & stand, yesterday, every moment hoping, & then every moment repining. I

---

1 Pearce–Carey Correspondence 1790–1828, Angus Library, Regent's Park College, University of Oxford. Italics original. Used by permission.

enquired of the residents in the parlor, "Pray have *you* a letter for me?" I repeated my question to the domestics in the kitchen—I applied to the warehouse—but all said "No.""Are you *sure*," I added, and could hardly believe them when they repeated their negative.

Ah, my dearest Sarah, said I as I lay in bed this morning marking the approach of day, O my Sarah what bids you cease to bless me? Are you so unkind—unkind, I said again hastily… No, that bosom is a stranger to unkindness. I must attribute either to accident or necessity the event which increases my pain. Well, thought I, however, *I'll* set a good example, it will be something to pledge when I visit Alcester again.[2] I'll e'en write today as usual. With this resolution I arose. But having a sermon to prepare for tomorrow evening & 3 besides for Sunday,[3] I imagined I should not be out of the path of duty were I to devote this day to my studies, & steal an hour tomorrow (at a friends where I am to dine) in order to acquit myself of inattention.

But the perusal of yours, which but a few hours since arrived, made me think ill of procrastination. You have heard before now, my love!, that on *some occasions* it is right to alter our resolutions, especially when it is for the best. & now, with a heap of loose papers around me—a fire almost extinguished near me—Miss Radford[4] attentively reading by my side & a large basin of a new sort of beverage called *Wassail* (made of ale, sugar, spice & roasted apples) before me (which Miss R has been so good as to make in order to gratify my curiosity) I have filled 2 thirds of my paper with nonsense to send you in return for yours which came fraught with enjoyment to me. But a mind like my Sarah's, knowing we are not at all time equaled fitted for epistolary intercourse,…I think I may make an apology extraordinary now, as it is near the hour of

---

2  Sarah lived in Alcester before her marriage to Samuel.

3  Evidently the Cannon Street Church held a Christmas Day service, which fell on a Saturday in 1790.

4  Miss Radford was a friend.

midnight. I have been racking my brains for ideas, arrangement &
illustration all day, and must either sit up some hours longer tonight
or resume the same employ early on the morrow.[5]

...PS. Should you write Mr. Summers ere I see you again, shall I
ask the favour of an affectionate remembrance to him? I rejoice in
the idea that you have heard from him. His friendship is highly
worthy of cultivation. I hope we shall both profit by it...

Adieu.

---

5 Although Pearce was a gifted preacher, a passage like this reveals that his
sermons took study and effort on his part.

# 5

## To his wife Sarah[1]

*Birmingham, December 2, 1791*

...I trust this will find you expecting a good Sabbath & waiting for the day of the Lord with ardent desires after his tabernacle—may your enjoyments equal your desires.

...Shall I advise my dear Sarah also to avoid any religious controversy with Mrs. Biggs.[2] I fear she has more studied system than yielded herself to the influence of truth. You, my love, I believe have been better employed. You cannot therefore enter the lists upon equal terms. You had better wholly decline. I have been much afraid lest she should distress your mind. I am under no apprehensions of her altering your sentiments. I believe you have been taught them by the Holy Ghost who dwelleth in you...and that you will be kept therein by the power of God.[3] But it will

---

1  The Samuel Pearce Mss., Angus Library, Regent's Park College, University of Oxford. Used by permission.

2  Mrs. Biggs appears to have embraced Socinian sentiments.

3  See 1 Peter 1:5.

pain your mind to hear your Lord degraded and the blood where-with you were sanctified accounted an unholy thing.[4]

My dear, my dearest Sarah—yours with sincere and ardent affection,

[S.P.]

---

4 See Hebrews 10:29.

# 6

## Friendship to Christ

*December 1791*[1]

The words [of John 11:11] present us with the real character of a true Christian, living. "Our *friend*," saith Jesus. Friendship is in itself a pleasing subject, both for reflection and discourse, especially pious friendship; that friendship to which our thoughts are now to be directed—friendship for Jesus Christ.

Friendship for Jesus Christ evidences itself, [first,] in a high esteem for his person. Lazarus, indeed, had opportunities of discovering his esteem for Christ, in a way which we have not... Was he persecuted in Jerusalem? He might go to Bethany—there he found

---

1 From Samuel Pearce, *Reflections on the Character and State of Departed Christians: In a Sermon, Occasioned by the Decease of The Rev. Caleb Evans, D.D.* (Birmingham: J. Belcher, 1791), 8–13. Pearce preached this funeral sermon on John 11:11 at Cannon Street Baptist Church on September 4, 1791, but he did not finish preparing it for the press till December 5, 1791. He was reluctant at first to publish it, but was prevailed upon by Birmingham friends of Evans, and he thus offered it to the public as "the tribute of an affectionate Pupil to the memory of a most worthy Tutor" (*Reflections on the Character and State of Departed Christians*, [3]).

Lazarus and his sisters ready to receive him, and afford a welcome shelter from the rage and malice of his foes. Did he stand in need of food, or lodging? Here he found attendance, so near approaching to unnecessary assiduity, as even to need restraint. Had his journeys occasioned his fatigue? Here the tears of affection flowed in torrents to wash his feet, whilst Mary neither thought it too mean to wipe them with the hairs of her head, nor too extravagant to anoint them with the most costly perfume. Did the rest of mankind reject his doctrines, and insult his person? Here he found Mary ready to sit at his feet, and listen to the gracious words which proceeded out of his mouth. No wonder Jesus loved Mary, and her sister, and Lazarus—no wonder Lazarus and his sisters loved Jesus.

But though we, my brethren, can no longer entertain this noble guest in person, yet, by entertaining the highest esteem for his character, and maintaining his personal honours, we may still prove our friendship.

When the Judean world despised Christ, and called him the carpenter's son, Lazarus and his sisters owned him as their Lord, and gave the most public proofs of their respect. Nor shall we, if we are true friends to Christ, be backward to avow his cause, and maintain his honours.

A man who thinks meanly of Christ, deserves not to bear his name. A mind enlightened into a knowledge of the gospel, cannot but revere him who shines throughout the whole as the brightness of the Father's glory, and the express image of his person.[2] He will be adored as "God over all, blessed for ever"[3]—trusted in as the great High Priest of the Christian profession[4]—and obeyed, as King in Zion, and sole legislator of his church.

With these views of Christ, is it possible his friend should be indifferent, while the majesty of his nature, the efficacy of his

---

2  Cf. Hebrews 1:3.

3  Romans 9:5.

4  Cf. Hebrews 3:1.

sacrifice, or the glory of his gospel, are publicly or privately opposed, or despised, by nominal professors? It is an insult to the sacred name of friendship to support it for a moment. Willing to endure the cross himself, the true Christian cannot bear without poignant grief, and holy zeal, to see his Saviour thus crucified afresh, and put to open shame.

In the present day...we have constant opportunities of seeking and supporting the dignity of the Son of God. In this age, perhaps above all others, those who call themselves his friends are most assiduous in lessening his honours, and insulting his character. Infidels and Deists have been outdone, or else see their efforts are needless. In the last age, the glories of Immanuel, God with us, became the sport of Atheists, or the ostensible ground on which the sons of Deism opposed Christianity—they have now quitted the field. Professing Christians, with the cross in their banners, have unsheathed the sword against the Lord of Glory, and Christ has been wounded in the house of his avowed friends![5] O how doth it behove us, if we are true friends of him, to abound yet more and more in all our zealous and scriptural efforts, to fight the good fight of faith, and contend earnestly for those glorious truths respecting the person of Jesus, which were, by himself, and his own apostles, delivered to the saints.

[Second,] friendship for Christ will discover itself also in a cordial, disinterested affection for his followers. Hence, saith Jesus, "*our* friend Lazarus." This good man did not confine his regard to Christ himself, but extended his kindness and care to his disciples too.

This has been since proposed as an indisputable evidence of real friendship for Christ: "By this we know we are passed from death unto life, because we love the brethren."[6] Pompous titles, splendid stations, unbounded wealth, extensive power or universal knowledge,

---

5 Is this a reference to the Antinomians whom Pearce had to battle in his own congregation?

6 1 John 3:14.

include the objects of worldly admiration, and direct the carnal heart where to place its friendship, and solicit its return. But a Christian, looking beyond the external glitter of wealth, and deaf to the noisy gust of vain applause, seeks the society, and cultivates the friendship of the disciples of the lowly Jesus—the man, and not the station, he admires—and justly thinks, "A Christian is the highest stile of man."[7] To select those whom Christ has selected, to lend assistance to those for whom his Redeemer bled, and to associate with those who are to be his companions for ever, will be his chief delight. In the Christian, he views Christ himself, and whether he meets him despised or applauded, abased or exalted, he will love the Christian for Christ's sake, and consider that whatever he does to the disciple, his master considers as done to himself.

[Third,] a true Christian, or friend to Christ, will be much concerned for, and do all his endeavour to promote, the cause and interest of Christ. Nothing affords him more joy than to hear of its success: like Barnabas, when he saw the grace of God at Antioch, he is glad;[8] and like Judah, rejoices when the salvation of the Lord comes out of Zion.[9] Whilst on the other hand, nothing gives him more pain than to hear of its decline. As David, so he can appeal to God, and say, "Lord, am I not grieved with those that rise up against thee? I count them mine enemies."[10]

A Christian's heart is interested, and the feelings of his heart will provoke the activity of his hands. His time, his powers, his fortune, yea, his life itself will be a sacrifice, small in his esteem, so that the cause of Christ may be promoted. "I count not my life dear," said

---

7 A quote from Edward Young, *The Complaint, or Night Thoughts on Life, Death and Immortality* (1742), "Night the Fourth. The Christian Triumph," line 750. Young's work was enormously popular in the eighteenth century and it appeared in a good number of editions.

8 See Acts 11:23.

9 Cf. Psalm 14:7.

10 Psalm 139:21–22.

Paul, "so I may fulfill the ministry I have received of the Lord."[11]

False are all those professions of friendship made by men, which cease in the day of adversity, or are suspended in the hour of necessity. The juvenile lawyer could call Jesus, Lord, and ask his instructions; but being told to part with his possessions for the sake of Christ's poor, he went away sorrowful, and thereby proved his insincerity.[12] Too many resemble him in the present day. They will call Jesus, Lord, but will afford no assistance to erect his kingdom, and even feel themselves unconcerned whether it prospers or declines. Let such remember, that indifferency of heart, or inactivity of life, respecting the cause of Christianity in the world, leaves no room to hope that they shall ever share its blessings. Let them not imagine they shall receive any thing of the Lord, for with what measure they mete, it shall be measured unto them again.

We have seen then, that only such as possess an high esteem for Christ, a cordial affection for his people, and manifest a zealous concern for his interest, can reasonably hope that Jesus will own them as his, and his people's friends, at a future day.

---

11 See Acts 20:24.
12 Cf. Mark 10:17–22.

*Bristol Baptist Academy*

BAPTIST COLLEGE & PRINCIPALS HOUSE, BRISTOL

# 7

## To a student at
## Bristol Baptist Academy[1]

### Birmingham, 1791

I greatly rejoice in your prosperity, both in concerns divine and scientific. Go on: and may the Lord bless you as a Christian, and as a Christian minister! It is certainly very proper that your public services should at present be curtailed as much as possible, as your continuance at the academy is uncertain. Probably you sometimes feel such a fervour of love to Christ and to souls, that you long to speak for one to the other; but let me advise you, when providence opens no way for your pouring out your soul *for* the Lord, to pour it out *before* the Lord. Private prayer will not retard your studies, but greatly assist them. Be much, very much, in this sweet, this profitable exercise.—Guard against an undue levity of disposition. I have suffered much for want of a more habitual restraint on

---

1 "Extracts of a Letter from Mr. Pearce to a Student at Bristol," *The Theological & Biblical Magazine,* 4 (1804): 125–126.

myself in this particular. Pray, and labour for seriousness. You know that I hate an affected gravity; but ministers ought to have no occasion to affect it; it should be habitual, and natural. I cannot but think, if I had laboured more for this at Bristol, that I should not have so much lamented its opposite at Birmingham. We do well to regulate the future by the experience of the past.

Do not lose a moment in gossiping, sleeping or in trifling conversation. Your time is truly precious. You cannot form a judgement of half the work you will make for repentance by present dissipation. I do not mean to say, use no exercise: but therein I exceeded. I wish you to gain by my loss.

I almost envy you your situation. Were I not satisfied of being in that place, about that business, and with those connexions which providence has directed me to, and still directs my continuance, I should gladly embrace an opportunity of becoming a humble student again, even though my place were the lowest on the lowest bench.

I am glad you love your tutors. Do not venture on too much familiarity with them; it would eventually excite in them disrespect for your person, and in you disrespect to their instructions. Strive to mingle the highest respect with the warmest affection. Yield to them in all things, except, where conscience may be concerned. Pay a manly deference to their judgement; never contradict, though you may not approve. Pray much for them, and for yourself.

Excuse me, if I have assumed the monitor too much. Had I not loved you much, I should not have been so free. You know who has said, "*Caritas omnia tolerat.*"[2]

S.P.

---

2 "Love endures all things," the Latin rendition of a portion of 1 Corinthians 13:7.

# 8

# *To Joshua Thomas*[1]

*Birmingham, December 21, 1792*

Rev. and dear Sir,

You request me to send you a "brief sketch of the character of my late dear friend and brother Mr. Josiah Evans, whilst he was at Bristol," nor will my affection for his memory or the pleasure I take in obliging you suffer me to refuse it. My acquaintance with him indeed was but of a short date, for we never saw each other till we met at the Academy, and he had not been there above 18 months before the ill state of his health obliged him to leave it, since which time I have never seen him but once.

---

1 From "Christian Friendship," *The Baptist Magazine*, 6 (1814): 101–104. The Welsh Baptist Joshua Thomas (1719–1797) was pastor of the Baptist cause in Leominster for forty-three years. For his life and thought, see Eric W. Hayden, *Joshua Thomas*, Part Two of Carroll C. and Willard A. Ramsey, eds., *The American Baptist Heritage in Wales* (Lafayette, Tennessee: Church History Research and Archives Affiliation, 1976).

Josiah Evans, about whom Pearce is writing in this letter, was one of Pearce's closest friends at the Bristol Baptist Academy. Evans never finished his studies but died in 1792. He was the nephew of Joshua Thomas. See "Rev. Josiah Evans, Brecknockshire" in Rippon, ed., *Baptist Annual Register*, 1:512–516.

But I had not long known him before I discovered that union of good qualities in his heart which commanded my affection and respect, and distinguished him as a proper person to select for the peculiar intimacies of pious friendship. Our apartments were adjoining; we spent most of the hour of relaxation together, and in a few weeks felt a mutual attachment. I believe I had more advantages for ascertaining his real character than either of our fellow students, for he was rather of a reserved disposition, and made sure of a friend before he had laid open his heart with any degree of freedom and confidence.

I found him possessed of an equable temper of mind, seldom agitated to an undue degree at the changing scenes around him, but steadily pursuing that object to which the maturest deliberation directed him. He was not hasty indeed in determining, but when he had once resolved he was generally inflexible. Perhaps he was too positive; but it is certain that an error here is not so injurious to a student as the opposite extreme. Resolutions hastily formed are in general as hastily abandoned; and minds disposed to these sudden revolutions cannot make those advances which attend a persevering application.

Mr. J. Evans had one essential qualification for friendship, and that was *faithfulness*. I believe he never discerned anything in my temper or conduct which he thought would be injurious to my proficiency as a student or to my spirituality as a Christian (after our intimacy commenced) but he watched for the first suitable opportunity of laying it before me with the reasons of his disapprobation. On some of these occasions he would urge his friendly admonitions and counsels with such affectionate eloquence that the result has been our retiring together with tears lamenting our mutual imperfections before God, and beseeching wisdom and grace from above to ornament our profession, and in every step to pursue something worthy of our being and character. Some of the moments we have thus spent I believe were marked with as true humiliation of heart as any we ever knew, for as we did not conceal the various states of our minds from each other; we had no occasion to restrain our feeling and guard our expressions in these exercises. On the contrary we felt as much freedom as though we had been apart and realized the presence of none but our Maker. "A world for *such a friend*, to lose, is gain."[2]

As a Christian, his views of evangelical truth were (according [to] my judgement) clear and consistent, his faith in them was without wavering, and the influence they had upon his heart and conduct was universal and permanent. He lived near to God. He watched over the state of his mind daily. I never found him unprepared for spiritual conversation. The things of God lay nearest his heart, and "from the abundance of the heart the mouth speaketh."[3] His letters abound in good and pious sentiment and I esteem the few I have in possession as "apples of gold in baskets of silver."[4] I never peruse them without some advantage, and by them, though dead, he yet speaks to me[5] and helps me to converse with him.

He bid fair for great usefulness in the *ministry*. A strong understanding, a becoming gravity of manner, an ardent desire for usefulness, a manifest tenderness for the interests of his hearers, and manly zeal for the glory of God, a general choice of the most evangelical subjects, together with a happy talent at introducing the figurative parts of Scripture to illustrate the subjects he discoursed on, were all united in his public services, and it is no wonder that he was generally acceptable to serious Christians. Nothing seemed wanting to make him eminently popular in England (for I hear he was so in Wales), but a more perfect acquaintance with the idiom of the language, and had it seemed good to the Head of the church

---

2  The origin of this saying is unknown.

3  Luke 6:45.

4  Cf. Proverbs 25:11. Pearce has changed the KJV's "pictures of silver" to "baskets of silver."

5  An allusion to Hebrews 11:4.

to have continued him a few years longer he would no doubt have filled up this deficiency, as his application was equal to his health, and his improvement to his application.

The removal of one who promised so much usefulness to the churches of God is among those mysteries of divine providence which call for the most unsuspecting confidence in the unerring wisdom and unchanging faithfulness of him who though "he giveth no account of any of his matters"[6] unto man, yet "doeth all things well."[7]

You, sir, are better acquainted of the particulars of my late friend's illness and decease than I am. It suffices that I have borne an honest though brief and imperfect testimony to his worth. I am happy in the confidence of your approbation from your personal acquaintance with this pious youth, and whilst I contemplate and admire his character I hope I can say "*Sequor*," although I must lament that it is "*non equis passibus*."[8]

I am, dear sir, with affectionate respect,
Your obliged friend and junior brother,
S. Pearce.

---

6  Job 33:13.

7  A loose quotation of Mark 7:37.

8  Pearce has omitted the "a" from the diphthong in "*aequis*." "*Sequor, . . . non æquis passibus*" is thus translated, "I follow, but not with equal steps."

# 9

## To his wife Sarah[1]

*Birmingham, May 31, 1793*

For the sake of my own peace I must suppose that my dearest Sarah arrived safe at her journey's end and for her sake I trust has experienced and expressed that gratitude to the God of all our mercies which stamps reality and sweetness on every enjoyment of life. O that I felt more of that myself, which I cannot but recommend to my best friends. Surely, if one of God's creatures hath more reason than another for praise, I am he. Indulged with bodily health—mental peace—domestic comforts—providential supplies—ministerial acceptance, usefulness, with the undissembled friendship of a crowd of the people of God—Lord, who and what am I to be so distinguished? We do pray for each other my dear S[arah]. Let us also praise for each other, specially since we have one common interest and the joys or griefs of one become by necessity the pleasure or pains of both.

---

1  "Pearce's Description of Carey's Farewell," *The Baptist Quarterly*, n.s., 1 (1922–1923): 386–387.

The evening of the day you left me was distinguished by feelings of the most rapturous pleasure, wonder and gratitude that my heart ever knew respecting the kingdom of God. Prepare my love, to rejoice and wonder and be grateful too! I received a letter from Dr. brother Ryland, and what d'ye think he wrote? Why Carey with all his family, are gone for India![2] When? How? you are ready to ask. I cheerfully satisfy you. Not long after the English fleet sailed, news came that a Danish East India Ship was to call at Great Britain in her way from Copenhagen to the East. Down came Thomas [and] Carey to Northampton at the news last Saturday.[3] Carey's wife (who was sufficiently recovered) offered to accompany him if her sister would go too.[4] The sister consented. They all set off for London together the same day. Carey wrote the Monday to Brother Ryland saying they had found friends in London who had advanced £200 above what the Society had in hand. That the sum was agreed on

---

2   Pearce is referring to William Carey, his wife Dorothy (1756–1807), and their family going out to India, where Carey would serve as a missionary. There were great difficulties in their going out to India, including England being at war with France, and Dorothy Carey's initial refusal to go to India. The whole family eventually sailed on a Danish ship. See Michael A.G. Haykin, *One Heart and One Soul: John Sutcliff of Olney, His Friends and His Times* (Darlington, Co. Durham: Evangelical Press, 1994), 198–235; Timothy George, *Faithful Witness: The Life and Mission of William Carey* (1991 ed.; repr. n.p.: Christian History Institute with Samford University, 1998), 66–93; John Appleby, *'I Can Plod…': William Carey and the Early Years of the First Baptist Missionary Society* (London: Grace Publications Trust, 2007), 80–106.

3   John Thomas was Carey's fellow missionary. On Thomas, see C.B. Lewis, *The Life of John Thomas* (London: Macmillan and Co., 1873).

4   Initially, Dorothy Carey did not want to go out to India. She was persuaded to do so when her younger sister Catharine Plackett agreed to go with her and her family to India. Dorothy's reluctance to support her husband has often been criticized, but it bears remembering that if she had ever travelled beyond her native Northamptonshire, it would only have been once or twice. Moreover, she had a very young family and was pregnant with a fourth child during the days leading up to the events described by Pearce. On the day she did agree to go, she spent time in prayer about the decision and was thus led to go with her husband. See S. Pearce Carey, *William Carey* (8th ed.; London: The Carey Press, 1934), 130. See also James R. Beck, *Dorothy Carey* (Grand Rapids: Baker Book House, 1992), 71–76.

*The house in Kettering, England, in which the Baptist Missionary Society (BMS) was formed on October 2, 1792*

with the Captain of the Ship, and the passage money paid down. That chaises were then at the door to convey Thomas to Portsmouth, to secure the baggage left there, and to take Carey and his family to Dover, from whence they were to embark. By this time I suppose they have sailed, and if the Lord prospers them will get to India time enough to receive Mrs. Thomas and the goods she has with her in the *Earl of Oxford*.[5] O what a wonder working God is ours! Tell the whole now if you please, for the honour of our Great Redeemer, and the encouragement of his people's faith in the most trying situations.

Three advantages are secured by the disappointment. First, the missionaries will go out more honourably and the enemies of the cause will not have it in their power to reproach the Society with publicity in transporting the missionaries under false pretences. Secondly, as the Danes are a neutral power there is no fear of their being captured by the French on their way. And thirdly, Carey has the satisfaction of his whole family, and the world have lost thereby an objection they have often raised to his going on the business.

… Do not delay writing if you have any concern for my satisfaction—I am, my dear S., your own very affectionate S. Pearce.

---

5  John Thomas' wife had sailed separately on an English ship, the *Earl of Oxford*.

# 10

## *To William Summers*[1]

*August 19, 1793*

My dear brother,

When I take my pen to pursue my correspondence with you, I have no concern but to communicate something which may answer the same end we propose in our annual journeys, *viz.* lending some assistance in the important object of getting and keeping nearer to God.[2] This, I am persuaded, is the mark at which we should be continually aiming, nor rest satisfied until we attain that to which we aspire. I am really ashamed of myself, when, on the one hand, I review the time that has elapsed since I first assumed the Christian name, with the opportunities of improvement in godliness which have crowded on my moments since that period; and when, on the other, I feel the little advance I have made! More light, to be sure, I have; but light without heat leaves the Christian half dissatisfied.

---

1 From Fuller, *Memoirs of the Rev. Samuel Pearce*, 27–29.

2 A reference to walking tours Pearce and Summers took annually in Wales. See Carey, *Samuel Pearce*, 111–112.

Yesterday, I preached on the duty of engagedness in God's service, from Jeremiah 30:21, "Who is this that engaged his heart to approach unto me? saith the Lord" (A text for which I am indebted to our last journey). While urging the necessity of heart-religion, including sincerity and ardour, I found myself much assisted by reflecting on the ardour which our dear Redeemer discovered in the cause of sinners. "Ah," I could not help saying, "if our Saviour had measured his intenseness in his engagements for us, by our fervency in fulfilling our engagements to him—we should have been now farther from hope than we are from perfection."...

Two things are causes of daily astonishment to me: the readiness of Christ to come from heaven to earth for me; and my backwardness to rise from earth to heaven with him. But, oh, how animating the prospect! A time approaches when we shall rise to sink no more: to "be forever with the Lord."[3] To be with the Lord for a week, for a day, for an hour; how sweetly must the moments pass! But to be forever with the Lord—that enstamps salvation with perfection; that gives an energy to our hopes, and a dignity to our joy, so as to render it "unspeakable and full of glory"![4]

I have had a few realizing moments since we parted and the effect has been, I trust, a broken heart. O my brother, it is desirable to have a broken heart, were it only for the sake of the pleasure it feels in being helped and healed by Jesus! Heart–affecting views of the cursed effects of sin are highly salutary to a Christian's growth in humility, confidence and gratitude. At once how abasing and exalting is the comparison of our loathsome hearts with that of the lovely Saviour! In him we see all that can charm an angel's heart; in ourselves all that can gratify a devil's. And yet we may rest perfectly assured that these nests of iniquity shall, ere long, be transformed into the temples of God; and these sighs of sorrow be exchanged for songs of praise.

---

3  1 Thessalonians 4:17.
4  1 Peter 1:8.

# 11

# To John Thomas and William Carey[1]

*Kettering, May 26, 1794*

...Many things have transpired since you left us, which I should have taken a pleasure in communicating, had you no other medium of intelligence; but brother Fuller has rendered this needless by

---

1 From *Missionary Correspondence: Containing Extracts of Letters from the Late Mr. Samuel Pearce, to the Missionaries in India, Between the Years 1794, and 1798; and from Mr. John Thomas, from 1798, to 1800* (London: T. Gardiner and Son, 1814), 3–7. John Thomas accompanied William Carey as a missionary to India in 1793. His character had a number of glaring faults—he was prone to mood swings, was easily angered, had little money-sense and was given to impatience—yet Andrew Fuller would later state after his death that his style of preaching was well suited for India ("Sketch of the Rev. John Thomas" in his *The Last Remains of the Rev. Andrew Fuller: Sermons, Essays, Letters, and Other Miscellaneous Papers, Not Included in his Published Works* [Philadelphia: American Baptist Publication Society, 1856], 326, 322–323). For a full-scale and balanced study of Thomas' life, see C.B. Lewis, *The Life of John Thomas* (London: Macmillan and Co., 1873). See also Michael A.G. Haykin, *A Cloud of Witnesses: Calvinistic Baptists in the 18th Century*, ET Perspectives, No. 3 (Darlington: Evangelical Times, 2006), 52–58.

the detail of occurrences which he is prepared to give you. And nothing is so tedious as a twice told tale. A few articles, however, he may have omitted, or if twice told may be of importance enough to forbid disgust.

Our Mission Society has been the means of provoking other Christians to love and good works. An Association is formed by the Independent brethren in Warwickshire for the propagation of the gospel in that country and, if possible, among the heathen too. It goes on with spirit and promises success. I preached a sermon for them about a fortnight ago from Gal 5:13, "By love serve one another," and put my people's generosity again to the test. It gave me pleasure to find that at the doors £11.14s.3d. was collected for them. I hope it will be a means of uniting us more firmly in the common cause. Another Association was formed December 11, 1793 at Kidderminster of seven churches in Worcestershire for the purpose of promoting evangelical truth and union. One of their resolutions is: "This Association shall be composed only of ministers and congregational churches in the county of Worcester, who profess Calvinistic sentiments and admit of free communion." Of these seven ministers, two are Baptists and five Independents.[2]

The resolutions both of the Warwickshire and Worcestershire Associations are in print. To the former is added a large extract from brother Carey's account of the state of the world etc. Were I at home I would send you a copy of both these publications, not doubting but you would derive considerable pleasure from a perusal. But I am now at Kettering, and preached for brother Fuller, who is in London, a successful pleader for the heathen and the Society formed for their spiritual advantage.[3] I will desire him to procure them for you in London, if possible, and hope he will succeed.

---

2  For more details, see Alan Argent, "The Founding of the London Missionary Society and the West Midlands" in Alan P.F. Sell, *Protestant Nonconformists and the West Midlands of England* (Keele, Staffordshire: Keele University Press, 1996), 15–18.

3  Fuller was in London, seeking to raise funds for the Baptist Missionary Society.

We have had a considerable work of God to rejoice in at Cannon Street the last winter. Many have been converted unto God and professed his name. Nor are other churches without occasion for praise: eight have been added at Arnesby,[4] twelve I baptized at Leicester, and seven more I hear are about to join the dear people in Harvey Lane soon.[5] A young man from our church at Birmingham has been preaching to them for above six months and has accepted an invitation for six more. He is generally approved and two of those baptized on the 20th of last month were called under his ministry.[6] The congregation also is upon the increase and the prospect is at present very encouraging. The sermon I preached on the morning of baptism, at the request of the church, is now in the press, but I fear will not be out time enough to admit the sending a few copies with this letter.[7]

At Walgrave there are near twenty young people under hopeful concern.[8] Some have been added at Northampton since brother Ryland has removed to Bristol, where he was formally settled the

---

4 Arnesby Baptist Church was where Robert Hall, Sr. had been pastor. When Hall died in 1791, he was succeeded by Thomas Blundel, Sr. (*c.*1752–1824), who pastored the church till 1804. On Thomas Blundel, see Haykin, *One Heart and One Soul*, 222–223.

5 Harvey Lane Baptist Church in Leicester, of course, had been Carey's church before he sailed for India in 1793. When Carey left the pastorate of this church, Pearce assumed the pastoral oversight—hence his baptism of the twelve new members. See Sheila Mitchell, *Not Disobedient... A History of United Baptist Church, Leicester Including Harvey Lane 1760–1845, Belvoir Street 1845–1940 and Charles Street 1831–1940* ([Leicester], 1984), 30–31.

6 It was Pearce who recommended to the Leicester congregation Carey's successor, a member of his own congregation, Benjamin Cave. For Cave's pastorate at Harvey Lane, see Mitchell, *Not Disobedient*, 30–37.

7 *The Scripture Doctrine of Christian Baptism; with Some Historical Remarks on that Subject* (1794 ed.; repr. Birmingham, 1806).

8 This is a reference to Walgrave Baptist Church, Northamptonshire, where Alexander Payne was the pastor at this time. Payne had been sent into the ministry from the Baptist cause at Bourton-on-the-Water during the pastorate of the celebrated Benjamin Beddome (1717–1795).

week before last. He is to spend some time with his friends at College Lane after the Association and I hear that seven candidates are waiting to receive baptism by his hands.[9] At Chenies too,[10] and at Earls Barton, where Mr. Shrewsbury was ordained over a congregation last Thursday,[11] and other places, the dear Redeemer's cause appears to be considerably advancing. What reason have we to praise the Lord and give thanks to his holy name!

I forgot whether Guilsborough meeting-house was destroyed by some incendiaries before you sailed or not. Be that as it may, a very good house, capable of containing six hundred people, was opened last Wednesday fortnight. Brother Sutcliff and I preached—I from "The wrath of man shall praise thee."[12] He, from "Save now, I beseech thee, O Lord: O Lord, I beseech thee, send now prosperity."[13]

9 Ryland had been the pastor of College Lane Baptist Church in Northampton before taking the post of Principal of Bristol Baptist College in 1793, a position that also entailed being the pastor of Broadmead Church. On Ryland, see pages 127–128, note 8.

10 The Baptist church in the village of Chenies, Buckinghamshire, had been constituted in 1760. Its minister during the 1790s was Nathan Sharman, from the Baptist cause at Arnesby, who was described by the London Baptist John Rippon as being "very industrious" (*The Baptist Annual Register* [London, 1798–1801], 3:5). By August 1796, the membership of the church stood at 74, which is quite remarkable given the size of the village. As Rippon commented, "Many attend the word in this village" (*Baptist Annual Register*, 3:5).

11 Earls Barton was a very familiar village to Carey since he had preached there once a fornight between 1782 and 1785. Thomas Shrewsbury was at Earls Barton less than two years. A John Timson was called to be pastor of this work in June 1796. See John Rippon, *The Baptist Annual Register* (London, 1794–1797), 2:481.

12 Psalm 76:10. It is interesting that Andrew Fuller also preached a sermon on this text in May 1794: see Joshua Wilson, *A Memoir of the Life and Character of Thomas Wilson, Esq., Treasurer of Highbury College* (London: John Snow, 1846), 125. According to Wilson, Fuller delivered this sermon on May 19, 1794, at Whitefield's Tabernacle in Moorfields, London. For an outline of Fuller's sermon on this text, see Joseph Belcher, ed., *The Last Remains of the Rev. Andrew Fuller* (Philadelphia: American Baptist Publication Society, [1856]), 186–187. Pearce's sermon on this text may well have suggested the text to Fuller. In fact, it might well be the case that Fuller also borrowed Pearce's outline.

13 Psalm 118:25.

*John Sutcliff (1752–1814)*

It was a solemn and delightful day. Brother Blundel preached at night from Judges 5:31; and I again, to above 200 people the next morning at five o'clock.[14] I recollect nothing more but what brother Fuller has written for your information already, and have therefore only to add the strongest assurances of my fraternal regard, and desire of hearing from you soon.

14 For details surrounding this event, see pages 24–26.

# 12

## On doing good

*Circular letter, June 11, 1794*[1]

Since it hath pleased an indulgent providence to favour us with the privilege of another interview with each other, we renew the usual token of our affectionate concern for your prosperity. It is matter of thankfulness to us that you yet exist as Christian societies; that the ordinances of God's house are continued to and enjoyed by you; and that, although some of our churches are complaining of unfruitfulness, others are in circumstances equally prosperous. It gives us pleasure, brethren, and we are persuaded that it will give you pleasure, to hear that the Lord is adding to his church of such as will be saved; but our pleasure is mingled with pain, because not all who profess have obeyed the gospel; some seemed to run well,

---

1 This circular letter of the Midland Baptist Association for 1794 was signed by Pearce and the other Association pastors on June 11. The title has been supplied by the editor since it is simply termed "Circular Letter, 1794" in the principal source for this text, namely, William Stokes, *The History of the Midland Association of Baptist Churches, From its Rise in the Year 1655 to 1855* (London: R. Theobald/Birmingham: John W. Showell, 1855), 115–121.

whose progress Satan hath hindered; and to preserve as far as we can the purity of our Societies, from such (according to the apostle's advice) we have withdrawn ourselves.[2] Yet, blessed be God, instances of this kind are comparatively few, and we hope they will be a useful warning to us all to "abstain from the appearance of evil," and to cry continually to God our strength, "Hold thou us up and we shall be safe."[3]

But, dear brethren, this is not the whole of our desire concerning you. To abstain from evil is but one trait in the Christian character; we are exhorted also to imitate our Divine Master, who went about doing good.[4] It should not satisfy us that we were once converted—that our conduct since hath been irreproachable—that God is faithful—and that heaven is secure. We should be frequently reviewing what present evidences we have of piety, and be aiming at a daily growth in grace. The doctrines of sovereign mercy were never designed to cherish our indolence, nor to make us happy in a state of spiritual sloth, and to use them for this purpose is in fact to abuse them. There is not one doctrine in the gospel but what is "according to godliness,"[5] nor one promise of future happiness unconnected with present holiness. Doth our Bible teach us the doctrine of God's everlasting love and his sovereign choice of his people? It declares also that they are "predestinated to be conformed to the image of Christ" and "are chosen through sanctification of the Spirit, and belief of the truth."[6] Doth the gospel announce the efficacious sacrifice of our blessed Redeemer on the behalf of sinners, and say, "He gave himself for us"? It is added "to redeem us from all iniquity, and to purify unto himself a peculiar people

---

2 See 2 Thessalonians 3:6.
3 Cf. 1 Thessalonians 5:22 and Psalm 119:117.
4 See 1 Corinthians 11:1; Ephesians 5:1–2; 1 Peter 2:21; and Acts 10:38.
5 1 Timothy 6:3.
6 Cf. Romans 8:29 and 2 Thessalonians 2:13.

zealous of good works."[7] Are we encouraged to expect the influences of the Holy Spirit? His office is to write the divine "law in our hearts and create us anew unto holiness."[8] Are we comforted with the delightful doctrine of the Perseverance of the Saints? That perseverance is described by the unerring word as a "continuance in well doing."[9] Finally, is life and immortality brought to light by the gospel? "He that hath this hope (it is said) purifieth himself even as God is pure."[10]

With these considerations before us we are anxious to discover in you, brethren, not merely an abstinence from iniquity, and an adherence to the sentiments we preach (this we rejoice in), but we are concerned that you "give all diligence to add unto your faith, virtue, and patience, and brotherly kindness, and charity, that you be neither barren nor unfruitful, but always abounding in the work of the Lord, pressing towards to the mark, for the prize of your high calling of God in Christ Jesus."[11] Happy shall we be, if by this address, or by any other means, we may stir you up to "forget the things which are behind, and to press after those which are before."[12]

To this end we beseech you first of all closely to examine into the real state of your souls. Christians should be very conversant with themselves. We hope that you have not prematurely entered on a religious profession; we trust that neither a speculative assent to the truths we maintain—a momentary transport of the passions —a fondness for the good opinion of others, nor a self-righteous dependence on the forms of religion, induced you to say, "we will go with you."[13] We entertain better hopes of you, brethren, and

---

7  Titus 2:14.
8  Cf. Jeremiah 31:33 and Ephesians 4:24.
9  Romans 2:7.
10 Cf. 1 John 3:3.
11 See 2 Peter 1:5; 1 Corinthians 15:58; Philippians 3:14.
12 Cf. Philippians 3:13.
13 Zechariah 8:23.

would take it for granted that you are Christians indeed, and that under the constraints of genuine love to Christ and his ways, you did publicly profess his name and espouse his cause.

But, dear brethren, in what state of mind are you now? Is your love any warmer—your faith any stronger—your hope more vigorous—or your humility more deep than when you first knew the Lord? Or have you, amidst all the obligations of saved sinners—all the ordinances of God's house—all the promises of the gospel, and the prospects of glory, been declining in your piety? Is it possible, that as your mercies multiply, your gratitude should abate; and that while you believe the Son of God loved you with an affection which "many waters could not quench, neither the floods drown"[14] you should cool in the ardour of your affection for him? Should this be the case, hear, we beseech you, the solemn address of Christ, first to the lukewarm Ephesians, and now to you: Rev. 2:4 and 5, "I have somewhat against thee, because thou hast left thy first love; remember, therefore, from whence thou art fallen, repent and do thy first works."

It will be profitable for you to examine into the causes of your declension! Have they not been irregularity in secret duties—an unnecessary association with unholy persons—too much eagerness in temporal pursuits—or the indulgence of a contentious or an unforgiving Spirit? These things, cherished or unrepented of, will as certainly injure our spirituality as strong poison without an antidote will disorder our bodies. The Spirit of God is an holy and a peaceful spirit; the indulgence of a temper or conduct dissimilar to his will grieve him and we shall be the losers. Reflect, brethren, how the degrees of our piety are connected with proportionate degrees of personal enjoyment, and general usefulness. When you lived nearer to God it was better with you than now and better for all around you. Your heavenly deportment put

---

14 Cf. Song of Solomon 8:7.

lukewarm professors to the blush, and stirred them up to fresh ardour in religion, whilst "like the sun when he goeth forth in his might"[15] you enlivened, encouraged and blessed all connected with you. And what excuse can any of us make for our spiritual dullness and inactivity? Is Jesus Christ less admirable than when we first beheld his glory, or are your obligations to him less than heretofore? Has investigation weakened the evidences of religion, or an experimental acquaintance with the gospel lessened our sentiments of its excellency? Hath God denied us a throne of mercy, or hath he ceased to be gracious?

Nay, brethren, we have only ourselves to accuse, let God and his throne be blameless. Surely it becomes us to "return unto the Lord—to take with us words, and say, O take away all iniquity, heal our backslidings, love us freely, and receive us graciously."[16] Heinous as our guilt hath been, he still is merciful. Still he bids us come, "Return ye backsliding children, and I will heal your backslidings, for I am married unto you, saith the Lord."[17] What gracious language! How calculated at once both to wound and heal, to convict and comfort, to reprove and to restore! To receive this address with a right spirit would be attended with deep humility and constrain us to acknowledge that all his ways are right, but ours alone are wrong, "for to us belongeth shame and confusion of face, but to him belongeth righteousness, because we have sinned against him."[18] With these sentiments let us look again to the cross of Christ—there we found relief at first and there alone we can obtain it now. A renewed application to Christ will produce more than regret for the past, it will stir us up to activity for the future; and indeed that hope of mercy which leaves the soul as languid as it found it, may and ought to be suspected as counterfeit and presumptuous.

---

15 Cf. Judges 5:31.
16 See Hosea 14:2, 4.
17 Cf. Jeremiah 3:14, 22.
18 Cf. Daniel 9:8.

"We beseech you, therefore, by the mercies of God, that ye present yourselves living sacrifices, holy, acceptable to God, which is your reasonable service."[19] Make a fresh surrender of yourselves to the Lord, and knowing that you are not your own property, but purchased by Immanuel's blood, strive to glorify him with "your bodies and spirits which are his."[20] Aim at obtaining an habitual sense of his omnipresence. Think and speak and act as in his sight. Watch over your spirits. Spend no idle time. Be ever doing something for God. Let no vain conversation proceed out of your mouth. Avoid foolish talking and jesting. Labour after a praying frame always, remembering that it is never well with us when we are unfit for prayer. Enter upon nothing in which you may not with propriety seek and hope to enjoy the approbation of your divine Master. Never engage in that which you are reluctant to consult God about, that reluctance proceeds from a suspicion that it is not pleasing to him, and we are told that whatever is not of faith is sin.[21] Be regular in the discharge of secret duties; why should everything in life have its stated seasons except personal religion? Think daily of our Lord's advice, "Labour not for the meat which perisheth, but for that which endureth to everlasting life."[22] And remember, it is in vain to call him Lord, unless we do the things he hath said.[23]

But brethren confine not your efforts to the improvement of your own hearts, be concerned for others also and endeavour to be public blessings. Have you families? Let not their blood be on your head. Converse frequently, affectionately and seriously with your servants and children on eternal subjects. Teach them to respect the Bible. Pray with and for them. Convince them that you have their good at heart and be careful that they see nothing in your temper

---

19 Cf. Romans 12:1.

20 Cf. 1 Corinthians 6:20.

21 See Romans 14:23.

22 Cf. John 6:27.

23 An allusion to Matthew 7:21.

or conduct, which you would not think becoming in theirs. Your advice will only be respected in proportion as it is followed with example. In your relation to the Church of Christ, be patterns to your brethren. Let your conduct as individuals be such as you think it would be right for all your fellow-members to imitate. Would it be right for all to be irregular in their attendance—to be seldom seen at social meetings for prayer—to be indifferent whether they afford pleasure to their ministers or break their hearts? If it is right for you, it is for all; but if not for all then it cannot be for you. We do most earnestly exhort you to pay the devoutest attention to the instructions given by our blessed Saviour, Matthew 18, "If thy brother trespass against thee, etc."[24] It is highly unbecoming to neglect the Lord's Table, as some do, through a slight disagreement with a fellow-member, when they have never taken a scriptural method to heal the breach; much worse is it to report a piece of misconduct to another before we have given the offender an opportunity for concession or repentance. Do in this, and all other cases, as you would be done by, and ever strive to deserve the characters of "The Sons of Peace."[25]

Pay attention to the state of the Congregation that meets with you. Be fellow-workers with us, as we hope we are with the Lord. It is true, the characters we sustain require a more habitual devotedness to the prosperity of Zion. We are engaged by every solemn obligation to give ourselves wholly "to prayer and the ministry of the word"[26]; but the work is great and requires the concurrence of all the friends of God. The souls of your families and of your neighbours are in some measure committed to your care. O let the perishing multitudes around you be precious in your eyes—think what Jesus Christ did to save souls and assist your Redeemer in realizing the fruit of his bloody passion and cruel death. Take every

---

24 Cf. Matthew 18:15.
25 An allusion to Matthew 7:12 and Luke 10:6.
26 Cf. Acts 6:4.

opportunity of bringing your careless acquaintance to hear the
Word of Life. And follow what we deliver in public with an affectionate personal application to their hearts. Tell them of their sad
estate as guilty sinners. "Save them, by plucking them out of the
fire."[27] Represent to them the infinite mercy of the Lord Jesus in
dying for mankind. Inform them of the guilt of neglecting his
salvation, and the happiness which attends a full surrender of the
heart to Christ. You, dear brethren, have "known the terrors of the
Lord"[28] and have "tasted also that he is gracious."[29] A recollection
of your own feelings will give an eloquence and energy to your
conversation, which, with the divine blessing, is likely above all
things to affect the heart. O, if all the members of our churches
were but to do all they might for God, what glorious days might
we expect to see! You remember it is said in the latter day that
"many shall run to and fro and knowledge shall be increased."[30]
What is this, but a prediction of the pious and successful activity
of real Christians to promote the cause of the dear Redeemer in
the world. If you are but stirred up to this activity, the prophecy
will begin to be accomplished—the captivity of Zion will be
drawing to an end, and Israel shall rejoice, and Judah shall be glad.
Should the Lord smile on your efforts and make each of you useful
to the recovery of one sinner from the error of his ways, who can
tell but he also in his turn may be useful to others—and they to
others—for ages yet to come, and so you may be channels through
which the blessings of salvation will flow to thousands to the end
of time. It may assist your determination to aim at promoting the
salvation of men to look back to your unconverted state. Perhaps,
awful thought, you may have been the means of provoking some
to sin and so have been instrumental to their everlasting

27 Cf. Jude 1:23.
28 Cf. 2 Corinthians 5:11.
29 Cf. 1 Peter 2:3.
30 Daniel 12:4.

perdition; and will you be less zealous in the cause of Christ than you were in the cause of Satan?

Let not shame or the fear of displeasing men withhold you from an attempt to lead sinners to Christ. They are not ashamed of their master and his cause, why should you be ashamed of yours? They are not backward to displease God in doing evil, why should you (through fear of displeasing men) be backward to do good? They spend their time in destroying their souls and the souls of others; why should you grudge a little time to save them? You may plead that you have not much understanding and know but little. If you are Christians, you know Christ and him crucified. We only exhort you to tell them what you do know. You would warn them if you saw their bodies in danger, why not when their souls (so much more precious) are on the point of ruin? Are you apprehensive they won't hear you? If "Israel be not gathered, yet shall you have your reward."[31] Jesus Christ had not much success in his personal ministry, yet he was not discouraged. He still persevered until "he brought forth judgement unto victory."[32] Have you but little time? It ought to be filled up the better. "Whatsoever your hands find to do for God, do it with all your might."[33] What reflections will afford you the most pleasure in a dying hour: that your light hath been put under a bushel or that it was placed upon a candlestick? Dear brethren, view this subject as you will view it at that solemn period. Where is the man who, in prospect of eternity, lamented that he had done too much for God? Thousands have wept because they had not done enough for him. Finally, think what pleasure it will give you at the judgement day to meet and spend eternity with some to whose salvation you have been instrumental; such a circumstance would add fresh energy to your joy, and lustre to your crown.

31 An allusion to Romans 11:7.
32 Cf. Matthew 12:20.
33 An allusion to Ecclesiastes 9:10 and Colossians 3:23.

Nor should your immediate neighbours only possess your affection, or engage your endeavours. A Christian's heart ought to be as comprehensive as the universe. The Asiatic, the American, and the African, as well as the European, have a claim on your philanthropy. Made of one blood, derived from one common ancestor, they are yet your brethren. Oceans and continents, though they forbid personal intercourse, do not make the relationship wider or the obligation less. In heaven you expect to join with happy spirits from every nation, kindred and tongue under heaven. Present difference in clime, or in colour, will form no distinctions there. "All souls are equal saith the Lord,"[34] and it is enough that a soul exists for a good man to use prayers and exertions for his salvation. Means are connected with ends, and when God, in his providence, gives being to the one, we may reasonably expect the other is at hand. Means are now used by our denomination, as well as others, to propagate the gospel among the heathen. We call you to "the help of the Lord against the mighty."[35] Has God given you the spirit of prayer? Forget not the ignorant and idolatrous, nor the men of God, who are gone to show them the way of salvation.

God has freely given you food and raiment for these twenty, forty, or sixty years, have you nothing to give to him who has given all to you? Nothing for him who became poor and shed his precious blood for you? Nothing for him who has promised heaven to you? Did Christ think souls so valuable that he laid down his life for their ransom, and are they to you so insignificant, that you cannot part with the superfluities of life for their sake? Can you bear to bestow that on fine clothes, or fine houses, or sumptuous entertainments, which might maintain a servant of Christ among the heathen? O, beloved, "if there be any consolation in Christ, if any bowels of mercy, fulfil ye our joy,"[36] and rather deny yourselves, than deny

---

34 An allusion to Ezekiel 18:4.
35 Cf. Judges 5:23.
36 Cf. Philippians 2:1–2.

poor sinners the means of obtaining to a knowledge of the Sariour. Consider what blessings you enjoy by the gospel! Did that man of God sacrifice too much who brought the news of a Redeemer first to England? And can you sacrifice too much to send those transporting tidings to Asia or Africa? God will fulfil his own word, and give "the uttermost parts of the earth unto his Son for his possession."[37] Let your love to Christ decide whether you shall be helpers in this glorious cause, or no.

Brethren, we live in an eventful age; nature appears almost in convulsions—kingdom rises up against kingdom, and nation against nation; these are signs of the times, and forewarn us that "the end of all things is hand."[38] "Watch ye, therefore, as those who wait for the Lord."[39] Have as little as possible to do with the world. Meddle not with political controversies, an inordinate pursuit of these (we are sorry to observe) have been as canker-worms at the root of vital piety, and caused "the love of many" (formerly zealous professors) "to wax cold."[40] The Lord reigneth! 'Tis our place to rejoice in his government, and "quietly to wait for the salvation of God."[41] The establishment of his kingdom will be the ultimate of all those national commotions which now terrify the earth.[42] "The wrath of man shall praise him, and the remainder of wrath he will restrain."[43] Attentive Christians may hear their Saviour's voice amidst all these desolating scenes, "Behold! I come quickly."[44] Happy for those who can confidently reply, "Amen, even so, come, Lord Jesus."[45]

---

37 An allusion to Psalms 2:8.

38 See Matthew 24:6-7; Mark 13:8; 1 Peter 4:7.

39 See Matthew 24:42; Mark 13:35; Luke 12:35

40 Cf. Matthew 24:12.

41 Cf. Lamentations 3:26.

42 An allusion to Revelation 19:15.

43 Psalm 76:10. Pearce had preached on this passage just over a month before he wrote this circular letter. See pages 25 and 92–94.

44 Revelation 22:7, 12.

45 Revelation 22:20.

Finally, brethren, farewell; be of good comfort, be of one mind; live in love, and the God of love and peace, shall be with you.

# 13

## *To William Summers*[1]

### *June 24, 1794*

We, my friend, have entered on a correspondence of heart with heart; and must not lose sight of that avowed object. I thank you sincerely for continuing the remembrance of so unworthy a creature in your intercourse with heaven; and I thank that sacred Spirit whose quickening influences, you say, you enjoy in the exercise. Yes, my brother, I have reaped the fruits of your supplications. I have been indulged with some reasons of unusual joy, tranquil as solitude, and solid as the rock on which our hopes are built. In public exercises, peculiar assistance has been afforded, especially in these three things: the exaltation of the Redeemer's glory; the detection of the crooked ways, false refuges and self-delusions of the human heart; and the stirring up of the saints to press onward, making God's cause their own, and considering themselves as living not for themselves, but for him alone.

---

1  From Fuller, *Memoirs of the Rev. Samuel Pearce*, 30–31.

Nor hath the Word been without its effect; above fifty have been added to our church this year, most of whom I rejoice in as the seals of my ministry in the Lord. Indeed, I am surrounded with goodness; and scarcely a day passes over my head but I say, "Were it not for an ungrateful heart, I should be the happiest man alive; and that excepted, I neither expect nor wish to be happier in this world. My wife, my children, and myself, are uninterruptedly healthy, my friends kind, my soul at rest, my labours successful, etc. Who should be content and thankful if I should not?" O my brother, help me to praise!

# 14

## To William Carey [1]

*Birmingham, August 9, 1794*

My very dear brother,

It was but a day or two after I had written my last letters that I had the inexpressible joy of receiving yours, dated Bay of Bengal and Calcutta. That moment more than compensated for all the anxieties which my affection for you, and concern for the prosperity of the good cause in which you have embarked, had created. Yes, the harvest already begins to be gathered in; and though, in some respects, I, with my brethren here, went forth weeping, now I bear my sheaves rejoicing in prospect of a still larger crop.[2] I need not acquaint you that last Monday the Committee, with other warm

---

1  From *Missionary Correspondence*, 11–13. As will be evident from the letters to Carey from Pearce in this volume, there was a deep friendship between the two men. Pearce attributed his missionary zeal to God's use of Carey's passion in this regard. As he told Carey, "We lighted our torch at yours, and it was God who first touched your heart with fire from his holy altar. To him be all the praise!" (Letter to William Carey, January 6, 1796 [*Missionary Correspondence*, 51–52]).

2  A reference to Psalm 126:5–6.

friends to the Mission, met at Guilsborough. Brother Fuller's letter will render all that information mere tautology. The accounts you gave us inspired us with new vigour and greatly strengthened our hands in the Lord. We read, and wept, and praised, and prayed.

O! who but the Christian feels such pleasures as are connected with friendship for our dear Lord Jesus Christ? Were there no hereafter, my dying breath should praise him for giving me a heart decidedly for him and his glorious cause on earth. May my whole life be spent for him! O! I feel, indeed I feel, that nothing is worth living for but his glory and the good of his Church. I hope I feel a daily conviction that I am a mere atom in creation, less than nothing, and vanity. Yet, with all my conscious meanness and unworthiness, I cannot help feeling myself dignified in my relation to the Son of God; and the highest ambition of my heart is to do something for him while I live.

There is no part of my life which I reflect on with so much pleasure as that which has been spent in behalf of the Society under whose patronage you are. And thrice happy should I be were the path of duty plain, if I could personally share the toils and pleasures of the Mission with you. At times I indulge a hope that my Lord will put me in a similar station; but then again I think, he well knows that I am inadequate to a task so arduous. Well, 'tis his to appoint; mine to acquiesce, submit and obey. I trust, whenever or wherever he calls, I shall have grace immediately to say, "Speak, Lord, for thy servant heareth."[3] It is our mercy, my brother, that he chooses our inheritance for us. He knows best our fitness for the various posts in his spiritual kingdom; and so that we are but where he would have us and doing what he bids us, we may rejoice in the common hope that he will at last say to us all, "Well done."[4]

---

3   1 Samuel 3:9.
4   Matthew 25:21, 23.

Last Lord's Day I read a part of your letter from the pulpit. It would have done you good had you seen the effects. It made the lame to leap as an hart, and caused the tongue of the dumb to sing! The following evening being the monthly prayer-meeting, a crowd of Christians came to testify their joy and gratitude. And you may assure yourselves that you have the prayers of the thousands of the Israel of God.

*William Carey (1761–1834)*

# 15

## To William Carey[1]

Birmingham, October 24, 1794

My dear, dear brother,

Never did I take pen in hand with such a combination of interesting feelings before. Love for your person, respect for your character, joy at your prospects, gratitude for your communications, desire for your success, and withal a hope that we shall yet meet in the flesh, so variously affect me that I can scarcely compose myself to write at all.

Blessed be the God and Father of our Lord Jesus Christ, who inclined your heart to undertake his cause among the heathen, a cause which European Christians may blush that they have neglected so long. But I hope the day is dawning when we shall all feel and sing as angels, "Peace on earth, and good will to men."[2] We have indeed been seeking every man his own things, not the things of others.[3] Ah, cursed self! How have Christians been bowing down

---

1 From *Missionary Correspondence*, 16–22.
2 Luke 2:14.
3 See Philippians 2:4.

to thy altar, forgetful that true philanthropy is a leading feature of that religion which they profess and of the character of him whose name they bear. We talk of morals, whilst our neglect of the duties of the second table too plainly demonstrate that we have imbibed but a small portion of the spirit of the first. We abide the greatest part of our lives beneath the power of the common lethargy. And if perchance a desire ever rises in our bosom for the good of others, we congratulate ourselves on our superior love for mankind, and doze, and doze, and doze again, whilst millions of immortal souls as precious as our own, drop into hell without an effort for their salvation.

Ah, whither is the apostolic spirit fled? Unlike the translated prophet who bequeathed a double portion of his spirit to his successor, the Apostle of the Gentiles and his contemporaries seem to have taken all their heroism, affection, zeal, greatness of design, and comprehension of effort with them to the skies, whilst we exist to gaze at what we scarce hope ever to obtain. But why? Where is the Lord God of Elijah? Where is the Lord God of Paul? Still he is near unto us, ready to animate with equal ardour the bosom of every faithful soldier who is willing to obey the injunctions of his Lord. You, my brother, have caught the falling mantle; but we in Europe are ready to ask, "Hast thou not a blessing for us also? Shall we not share the pains and pleasures, the conflicts and the conquests of our distant brethren? Who denies us the privilege? What forbids our standing in the same rank with them and enjoying the honour of the foremost in the charge of Immanuel's troops upon the infernal powers among the heathen?"

Brother, I long to stand by your side and participate in all the vicissitudes of the attack, an attack which nothing but cowardice can make unsuccessful. Yes, the Captain of our salvation marches at our head. Sometimes he may withdraw his presence, but not his power, to try our process with our spiritual arms and celestial armour. O what cannot a lively faith do for the Christian soldier!

It will bring the deliverer from the skies; it will array him as with a vesture dipt [*sic.*] in blood; it will place him in the front of the battle and put a new song into our mouths: "These made war with the Lamb but the Lamb shall overcome them."[4] Yes, he shall; the victory is sure before we enter the field. The crown is already prepared to adorn our brows, even that crown of glory which fadeth not away[5]; and already we have resolved what to do with it. We will lay it at the conqueror's feet and say, "Not unto us, O Lord, not unto us, but to thy name give glory,"[6] while all heaven unites in the chorus, "Worthy the Lamb."[7]...

Neither of us has forgot a conversation a little before you left us on the exercises of my mind respecting an effort for the spread of the gospel in foreign lands, which for ten years now have more or less attended me. I cannot forget your prediction with which the conversation ended, "Well, you will come after us." From that time to the present, the desire has been increasing with scarce any intermission, except when spiritual things have been at a low ebb with me. But for several weeks past I have been too full to contain, and I resolved to come to a point either about going or staying. For this purpose, I first attentively considered my situation in every relation at home and the duty of ministers arising from the general commission of our Lord,[8] together with the disproportion of means to the multitude of mankind. And I concluded that it was my duty to join hands with you in your great and laudable undertaking. I expected opposition from many quarters. I thought I would take every prudent step to know the mind of God. ...

[I] therefore, secondly determined that, after setting apart a certain day in every week for some weeks on purpose to pray with

---

4 Revelation 17:14.
5 See 1 Peter 5:4.
6 Psalm 115:1.
7 Revelation 5:12.
8 A reference to Matthew 28:19–20.

fasting to God for his direction and examining the matter on every side, I would, if the same views remained or were confirmed, lay the case before the Society and leave it with them to decide, resolving in the strength of God to abide by their judgement.[9] The time I proposed to wait is now nearly expired. I have met with heart-breaking trials of a domestic nature since I made known my inclination; but I thank God I faint not, and every day more fully convinces me that I ought to go. Now as I mean to adhere to my plan, I have not yet acquainted the Society with my views. There is a meeting at Roade on the 12th of November, 1794. That opportunity I intend to embrace, God willing, and then whether my Master will count me worthy of so high a calling, or whether his providence may check my temerity, will be determined.

I wish I had time to delay sending this letter till that period is past; but the ship sails in a few days and I was unwilling that you should be unacquainted with the state of my mind. I have reason to be thankful that, notwithstanding I have been severely tried from quarters the most afflictive, yet I never enjoyed so much of God since I have been in the ministry. Where no friend would or could sympathize with me, I have found him ever nigh. And yesterday my wife told me that on mature deliberation she approved of the plan I have adopted, and was much more comfortable in her mind than ever before since she knew my wishes, and was willing to leave it to the judgement of the ministers as I proposed, hoping she would see it in the hands of God. O help me to praise! It is a relief inexpressible. If I come, I am not without hopes of a companion in the good work.[10]

---

9  For this time of searching for the will of God, see pages 27–32.

10 A reference to Sarah Pearce. Pearce would have known of Dorothy Carey's initial reluctance. See page 84, especially notes 2 and 4.

# 16

## To William Rogers[1]

Birmingham, October 27, 1794

My very dear friend,

It is certainly as impossible for Christians to maintain a pious intercourse without Love, as for the magnetic needle to point any where but to the pole. Condemn me not then, if I address you in a less distant form than heretofore. ...

In situation, in publicity of character, in mental vigour, in age, in literary acquirements, in a thousand things we may differ, but still we are one in Christ Jesus, that dear centre of union to holy angels and holy men—to perfect saints above, and imperfect saints below. Allow me then, in the exercise of that delightful, godlike grace

---

1  From "Original Letters, of the Rev. Samuel Pearce," *The Religious Remembrancer* (October 22, 1814): 29. A portion of this letter can also be found in *The Theological & Biblical Magazine*, 4 (1804): 218–220. William Rogers was pastor of the First Baptist Church in Philadelphia from 1772 to 1775, and then Professor of Oratory and the English Language at the University of Pennsylvania till 1811. See the "Biographical Sketch of William Rogers, D.D.," *The New Baptist and Evangelical Repository* 1 (1825): 1–3.

which has the precedence even to that faith which is unto salvation, and that hope which fastens upon immortality, to throw the
arms of my affection across the Atlantic, and embrace you as a
beloved brother in the Lord—yes, you will allow it; and you will
not disdain my youth nor want of name; you will regard me as
participating of his paternal regards "of whom the whole family
in heaven and earth is named"[2]—you will pardon my imperfections—give me the right hand of fellowship, and say, "affection
without rudeness, I will never censure."

...I love that man who tenderly feels for the souls of the poor
heathen. What a reflection on the philanthropy of every Christian
country is it that no more pains have been taken to carry the light
of eternal life to those nations who "sit in darkness and in the
shadow of death"[3]? What a lapse of time since the Reformation;
but how little hath its wasting years been improved to this important end? We and our fathers have thought and spoke, and written
and heard, and read about Christian benevolence; we have investi-
gated its nature; we have admired its beauty; we have contended for
its importance to the Christian character, whilst, like the unap-
proved servant, though we knew our master's will, we did it not[4]:
almost the whole Christian world have partaken of the common
lethargy, and if a few here and there have thought about the state
of pagan nations, and felt a faint desire for their salvation, or at most,
mentioned the "ingathering of the Jews and the fullness of the
Gentiles,"[5] as a thing of course in their prayers, they have felt a
self-complacency on account of their superior zeal (comparing

2 Ephesians 3:15.
3 Luke 1:79.
4 See Luke 12:42–48.
5 An allusion to the eschatological perspective based on Romans 11 that prior
to the second coming of Christ there would be a great converting work of the
Holy Spirit among the Jewish people. See Iain H. Murray, *The Puritan Hope. A Study
in Revival and the Interpretation of Prophecy* (Edinburgh: The Banner of Truth Trust,
1971).

their feelings, not with the greatness of the subject, but the feelings of their yet more lethargic neighbours) have satisfied themselves without any positive exertions, and lain down dozing—dozing, dozing at their ease, whilst thousands of immortal souls, as precious as their own, have been daily dropping into hell without one effort made for their salvation?—But the time is come, I hope, when we shall every man look no longer at his own things only, but the things of others: Zion already travails in birth, and soon she shall bring forth her children;—already heaven is besieged with earnest supplications[6]; they who make mention of the Lord keep no longer silence; they will "give him no rest until he makes Jerusalem a praise over all the earth."[7]

A missionary spirit seems now to prevail among serious Christians of every denomination in Great Britain; the tidings from our missionaries in Asia, will add fuel to the holy fire.[8] The Independent brethren are already associating for this purpose.[9] It will not be long before "many will run to and fro and knowledge shall be increased,"[10] even the knowledge of "the true God and Jesus Christ whom he hath sent, whom to know is eternal life."[11]...

P.S. ...I have been hoping that whilst the United States are forming societies for the encouragement of arts, liberty and emigration,

---

6 This is a reference to the monthly concerts of prayer for revival that had marked Baptist life since 1784 and that also involved prayer for missionary advance. See Haykin, *One Heart and One Soul*, 153–171.

7 Cf. Isaiah 62:7.

8 William Carey, John Thomas and the Baptist mission in India.

9 In 1795, the Independents, or Congregationalists, formed the London Missionary Society (LMS). Pearce had strong friendships with Independent ministers in the Midlands and played a role in the formation of the LMS. See Alan Argent, "The Founding of the London Missionary Society and the West Midlands" in Alan P.F. Sell, *Protestant Nonconformists and the West Midlands of England* (Keele, Staffordshire: Keele University Press, 1996), 15–18.

10 Daniel 12:4.

11 Cf. John 17:3.

there will, ere long, be found a few who will form a society for the transmission of the word of life to the benighted heathen— may not such an event be hoped for? Or, if a new society should be thought inexpedient, perhaps they may strengthen their brethren in Europe, by some benevolent proofs of concurring with us in a design which so many on both sides the water profess so much to approve.[12]

---

12 Pearce's wish would be realized in 1812 when the American Board of Commissioners for Foreign Missions sent the first American Protestant missionaries, Adoniram (1788–1850) and Ann Judson (1789–1826), Luther Rice (1783–1836), and Samuel (1785–1841) and Harriet Newell (1793–1812) to Asia. The Judsons and Rice became convinced of believer's baptism during their voyage to India and were baptized by William Ward in Calcutta.

# 17

## To his wife Sarah[1]

### *November 13, 1794*

My dear Sarah,

I am disappointed, but not dismayed. I ever wish to make my Saviour's will my own. I am more satisfied than ever I expected I should be with a negative upon my earnest desires, because the business has been so conducted that I think (if by any means such an issue could be ensured) the mind of Christ has been obtained. My dear brethren here have treated the affair with as much serious-ness and affection as I could possibly desire, and I think more than so insignificant a worm could expect. After we had spent the former part of this day in fasting and prayer with conversation on the subject till nearly two o'clock, brother Potts, King[2] and I retired.

---

1 From Fuller, *Memoirs of the Rev. Samuel Pearce*, 52–53.

2 Thomas Potts (d.1831), a local merchant, and Thomas King (1754–1831), a grocer by trade, were two of the deacons at Cannon Street Baptist Church. Potts had helped provide William Carey with the finances to print his missionary classic *An Enquiry into the Obligations of Christians, To Use Means for the Conversion of the Heathens* (1792 ed.; repr. Didcot, Oxfordshire: The Baptist Missionary Society, 1991).

We prayed, while the committee consulted. The case seemed difficult, and I suppose they were nearly two hours in deciding it. At last, time forced them to a point, and their answer I enclose for your satisfaction. Pray take care of it; it will serve for me to refer to when my mind may labour beneath a burden of guilt another day. I am my dear Sarah's own, S.P.

---

For more information on Potts, see Carey, *William Carey*, 56–57, 87. For further information on both Potts and King, see Carey, *Samuel Pearce*, 115–116 and Ernest A. Payne, *The First Generation: Early Leaders of the Baptist Missionary Society in England and America* (London: Carey Press, 1936), 60–67. For a list of the deacons at the church, see "A List of the Particular Baptist Churches in England, 1798" in Rippon, ed., *Baptist Annual Register*, 3:34, note★ 300.

# 18

## *To his wife Sarah*[1]

*Northampton, December 13, 1794*

My dear Sarah,

I am just brought on the wings of celestial mercy safe to my Sabbath's station. I am well, and my dear friends here seem healthy and happy; but I feel for you. I long to know how our dear Louisa's pulse beats; I fear still feverish.[2] We must not, however, suffer ourselves to be infected with a mental fever on this account. Is she ill? It is right. Is she very ill....dying? It is still right. Is she gone to join the heavenly choristers? It is all right, notwithstanding our repining. ....Repinings! No; we will not repine. It is best she should go. It is best for her; this we must allow. It is best for us; do we expect it? Oh what poor, ungrateful, short–sighted worms are we! Let us submit, my Sarah, till we come to heaven; if we do not then see that it is best, let us then complain.

But why do I attempt to console? Perhaps an indulgent providence has ere now dissipated your fears; or if that same kind

---

1 From Fuller, *Memoirs of the Rev. Samuel Pearce*, 80–81.
2 A reference to Louisa Pearce (1792–1809), the eldest of the Pearces' children.

providence has removed our babe, you have consolation enough in him who suffered more than we; and more than enough to quiet all our passions in that astonishing consideration, "God so loved the world, that he *spared not* his own Son."[3] Did God cheerfully give the holy child Jesus for us; and shall we refuse our child to him? He gave his Son to suffer; he takes our children to enjoy. Yes; to enjoy himself.

Yours with the tenderest regard, S.P.

---

3 John 3:16; Romans 8:32.

# 19

## *To William Carey*[1]

*Birmingham, March 27, 1795*

My very dear brother,

Instead of a letter, you perhaps expected to have seen the writer;
and had the will of God been so, he would by this time have been
on his way to Mudnabatty.[2] But "it is not in man that walketh to
direct his steps."[3] Full of hope and expectation as I was, when I
wrote you last, that I should be honoured with a mission to the
poor heathen and be an instrument of establishing the empire of
my dear Lord in India, I must submit now to stand still and see
the salvation of God. Judging from the energy of my feelings,
together with their long continuance and growing strength, I scarce
entertained a doubt but I should this year go to assist you in your
evangelical undertaking, and under those circumstances I wrote to
you. It was not long after, that some of our church, guessing from
the strain of my preaching at the state of my mind, questioned me

---

1 From *Missionary Correspondence*, 26–31.
2 Also spelt Mudnabati.
3 Jeremiah 10:23.

upon the subject, and I frankly told them all my heart. On this, various meetings of consultation were held and I suffered much, but fainted not. And during that struggle, I felt, for the first time, the plenary import of that phrase, "The world is crucified unto me, and I unto the world."[4] No domestic attachment, nor flattering prospects of reputation, nor wealth, which in unworthier moments have had too much ascendency over me, had now any influence. Love to Christ and love to sinners, heathen sinners, reigned triumphant in my soul, and I trust I did then feel what it was to be wholly devoted to God.

At length, a full church meeting was called, and I was requested to be present. I went accordingly, and having stated my views and feelings, I told them that though I should be glad of their opinion, yet I should not think myself bound to abide by their decision, because their affection for me would incline them to partiality in their judgement. I then withdrew.

The issue of the meeting was unfavourable to my going, and as I had expressed my design of finally submitting to the opinion of a meeting of disinterested ministers, the church appointed two of the deacons to represent them at this meeting, whenever it should be. In the meantime I laid the case before three or four of our brethren, whose piety and experience I thought best enabled them to judge. I was both disappointed and grieved to find them all decidedly against me. The following is an extract from one beloved brother and father in the ministry.[5]

---

4  Galatians 6:14.

5  This was Abraham Booth (1734–1806), a highly esteemed London Baptist minister. Fuller once referred to him as "the first counselor" of the Baptist denomination. See Ernest A. Payne, "Abraham Booth, 1734–1806," *The Baptist Quarterly*, 26 (1975–1976): 28. On Booth, see especially John Rippon, *A Short Memoir of the Rev. Abraham Booth* in James Dore, *A Sermon, Occasioned by the Death of The Rev. Abraham Booth, Preached in Little Prescot Street, Goodman's Fields…: And A Short Memoir of the Deceased, Incorporated with The Address Delivered at His Interment…by John Rippon* (London, 1806), 41–98; William Jones, *Essay on the Life and Writings of the Rev. Abraham*

*To William Carey*

I really think you must not leave England. The heathen will get more by you here than they will abroad; and surely your post must not be given up. Who is there in your neighbourhood to make a stand against false religion, my dear brother? I bless God for the zeal, but surely I think it will hurt the cause in various ways if you go. Churches will be afraid of the consequences of encouraging missions, if the most important stands at home are deserted by those that God has greatly prospered in them. You know brother Fuller's infirmity.[6] If you run away, we shall want a man too of activity to keep alive the attention of the public to the cause and give a great argument to them that are averse to it. I am pleased with the measures you propose to follow for determining the point, and trust God will direct you.

I copy out this just as I received it, that you may better enter into my situation. The week after this we had a very solemn day of fasting and prayer on the business at Northampton.[7] Some brethren of the Society, and some who were not, attended. Brethren Ryland and Sutcliff were not able to be present,[8] but their minds

---

Booth (Liverpool, 1808); Payne, "Abraham Booth," 28–42; Robert W. Oliver, "Remembering Abraham Booth (1734–1806)" in Michael A.G. Haykin with Alison E. Haykin, eds., *The Works of Abraham Booth* (Springfield, Missouri: Particular Baptist Press, 2006), I, 1–24; Raymond Arthur Coppenger, *A Messenger of Grace: A Study of the Life and Thought of Abraham Booth* ([Kitchener,] Ontario: Joshua Press, 2009); and Michael A.G. Haykin, ed., *"The First Counsellor of our Denomination": Studies on the Life and Ministry of Abraham Booth (1734–1806)* (Springfield, Missouri: Particular Baptist Press, 2011).

6   This is a reference to a small stroke that Fuller suffered in 1793.

7   See page 29.

8   John Ryland, Jr. and John Sutcliff (1752–1814) were two of Pearce's closest friends and central figures in the formation of the Baptist Missionary Society. Both also wholly shared Andrew Fuller's evangelical Calvinism. Ryland pastored with his father, John C. Ryland in Northampton for a number of years before moving to

were known, together with some of the London ministers. On this occasion I read a diary of my feelings for some time past together with the views and motives which induced me to desire employ-ment among the heathen and such answers to objections arising from my connexion in the family, the church, and the Mission Society, as appeared to me satisfactory and full. I shall ever love my dear brethren the more for the tenderness with which they treated me and the solemn prayer they repeatedly put up to God for me.

At last, I withdrew for them to decide, and whilst I was apart from them and engaged in prayer for divine direction, I felt all anxiety forsake me and an entire resignation of will to the will of God, be it what it would, together with a satisfaction that so much praying breath would not be lost; but that he who hath promised to be found of all that seek him would assuredly direct the hearts of my brethren to that which was most pleasing to himself and most suitable to the interests of his kingdom in the world. Between two and three hours were they deliberating after which time a paper was put into my hands, of which the following is a copy.

The brethren at this meeting are fully satisfied of the fit-ness of brother P's qualifications and greatly approve of the disinterestedness of his motives and the ardour of his mind. But another missionary not having been requested, and

---

Bristol in 1793, where, until his death in 1825, he was the pastor of Broadmead Church and the principal of Bristol Baptist Academy. Sutcliff was the pastor of Olney Baptist Church, Buckinghamshire, from 1775 until his death in 1814.

On both men, see Haykin, *One Heart and One Soul*, *passim*. See also Michael A.G. Haykin, " 'A Habitation of God, Through the Spirit': John Sutcliff (1752–1814) and the revitalization of the Calvinistic Baptists in the late eighteenth century," *The Baptist Quarterly*, 34 (1991–1992): 304–319 and *idem*, "John Ryland, Jr.—'O Lord, I would delight in Thee': The life and ministry of John Ryland, Jr. appreciated on the 250th anniversary of his birth," *Reformation Today*, 196 (Nov-Dec 2003): 13–20.

not being in our view immediately necessary, and brother P. occupying already a post very important to the prosperity of the Mission itself, we are unanimously of opinion that at present, however, he should continue in the situation which he now occupies.

To this I was enabled cheerfully to reply, "The will of the Lord be done." And receiving this answer as the voice of God, I have, for the most part, been easy since, though not without occasional pantings of spirit after the publishing of the gospel to the pagans.

# 20

## The doctrine of salvation by free grace alone

*May 27, 1795*[1]

Dear Brethren:

With gratitude to the great Master of assemblies for another pleasing interview with each other, we unite in expressing our most affectionate wishes that you also may be comforted, with the same consolations "wherewith we ourselves have been comforted of God."[2] On this side [of] heaven, indeed, we must not expect our

---

1 This circular letter was drawn up by Pearce for the annual association meeting of the Midland Association on May 26–27, 1795. It has been reprinted a number of times since then. The Philadelphia Baptist William Rogers and William Staughton (1770–1829), who had been baptized by Pearce and was one of the founding members of the Baptist Missionary Society, had it reprinted in 1803: *Circular Letter of the Elders and Messengers of the Several Baptist Churches Met in Association at Bewdley, in Worcestershire, England* (Burlington: Stephen C. Ustick, 1803). It was also reprinted again in 1855 by the New York Baptist Association and in 2004 by *The Founders Journal* 57 (Summer 2004): 26–33.

2 2 Corinthians 1:4.

pleasures to be wholly undisturbed; yet, possessed of that faith which overcometh the world, we would exclaim with the holy apostle, "Thanks be unto God, who always causeth us to triumph in Christ," and teacheth us, to "glory in tribulations also."[3]

Some causes of grief have been suggested in the various epistles from the churches.[4] Among these, in some places, the want of success in bringing souls to Christ; in others, the little zeal and diligence which appear in professors; the death of some and the unbecoming conduct of others have been lamented. But, brethren, these are trials from which no age of Christianity, not even the apostolic, has been exempted. Let not these things discourage us. He that laid the foundation of his church, will build her up; he will not desert the work of his own hands, and though Zion may complain, "The Lord hath forsaken me!" it will not be long before he will prove to her joy, that she is "engraven on the palms of his hands, and that her walls are continually before him."[5] It shall yet be said, "Cry out and shout, thou inhabitant of Zion, for great is the Holy One of Israel in the midst of thee."[6] Amidst our causes of complaint, we are not without some indications of the divine favour: some of our churches have enjoyed very comfortable additions; most are in peace; and some, who were last year destitute of pastors, are now agreeably supplied. Nor is it one of the least causes of our joy that our various congregations still avow their attachment to the Faith once delivered to the saints.

The point of difference between us and many other professing Christians lies in the doctrine of salvation entirely by grace. For whilst some assert that good works are the cause of justification;

---

3   2 Corinthians 2:14; Romans 5:3.

4   Each church in the Association would send a letter to the annual meeting describing the church's experience through the previous year and the church's present situation.

5   Cf. Isaiah 49:16.

6   Isaiah 12:6.

some that good works are united with the merits of Christ and so both contribute to our justification; and others that good works neither in whole nor in part justify, but the act of faith; we renounce everything in point of our acceptance with God, but his free grace alone which justifies the ungodly, still treading in the steps of our venerable forefathers, the compilers of the *Baptist Confession of Faith*, who thus express themselves respecting the doctrine of justification: "Those whom God effectually calleth, he also freely justifieth,...for Christ's sake alone; not by imputing faith itself, the act of believing, or any other evangelical obedience to them as their righteousness; but by imputing Christ's active obedience unto the whole law, and passive obedience in his death for their whole and sole righteousness, they receiving and resting on him and his righteousness by faith" which "is the alone instrument of justification."[7]

In this point do all the other lines of our confession meet. For if it be admitted that justification is an act of free grace in God without any respect to the merit or demerit of the person justified, then the doctrines of Jehovah's sovereign love in choosing to himself a people from before the foundation of the world, his sending his Son to expiate their guilt, his effectual operations upon their hearts, and his perfecting the work he has begun in them until those whom he justifies he also glorifies, will be embraced as necessary parts of the glorious scheme of our salvation.

At this doctrine, therefore, hath the chief force of opposition been directed, and various are the modes in which it has been attacked: sometimes by appeals to our passions, then to our reason, and at other times to the Scriptures. We hope, brethren, you are too well read in your Bible to be at a loss for weapons of defence against the assaults, since whatever the passions or opinions of men may plead, those holy oracles assure us that we are "justified freely by

---

7 *The Second London Confession of Faith* 11.1–2 in William L. Lumpkin, *Baptist Confessions of Faith* (Rev. ed.; Valley Forge, Pennsylvania: Judson Press, 1969), 265–266.

the grace" of God and that he hath mercy on whom he will.[8] But there is another mode of attack, as frequently and vigorously pursued as either of the former. It is asserted that our doctrine "involves in it conclusions inconsistent with religion, both natural and revealed, that it gives an unjust and offensive idea of God, that it relaxes the obligations of men to faith and holiness, that it withholds consolation from penitent sinners, and saps the foundations of true morality in the world." These are serious charges, and if they can be substantiated, we shall do well to exchange our creed for a better; but let us examine with what propriety such consequences are charged on our profession.

First, because we maintain the free salvation of God's elect, we are accused of holding the doctrine of "the absolute reprobation of all the rest of mankind, so as to involve in it this horrible consequence, that God creates innumerable souls to be inevitably damned without the least compassion for them." That to choose some implies to leave others must be granted; and if nothing more were meant by the charge of free election involving in it the doctrine of reprobation, we should not object to the statement. But is there no difference between leaving men to the just fruit of their sins and creating them for inevitable damnation irrespective of their characters? We cheerfully avow our abhorrence of a doctrine which asserts that an infinitely good God created a number of immortal beings capable of such strong sensations of misery as man merely to gratify himself in filling them with the fullness of torment for ever. Such a sanguinary deity we could never love. Nor would faith in such a being promote that disposition to gentleness, tenderness and affection for all mankind, which are everywhere represented in the gospel as the genuine fruits of a spiritual acquaintance with the true character of God. On the contrary, such views of the Almighty would rather cherish the spirit of a bloody Mohammed than a bleeding Jesus.

---

8  Romans 3:24; 9:15–16.

But we conceive that our detestation of such a creed is no ways inconsistent with our cordial assent to the doctrine of the sovereignty of divine mercy. For as the execution of a malefactor is not to be attributed to the cruelty of a prince because royal clemency is displayed towards transgressor, so neither do the sovereign acts of God's mercy in any respect necessitate him to be the author of misery any farther than as the author of that holy law which men have broken and the maintaining of its rights.

In saving, he acts like a merciful sovereign; in condemning, as a righteous judge, bound to support the honour of his moral government. He was no more under obligation to save all, than he was to save any; and if salvation itself be an act of grace, surely the author of salvation is at full liberty, without any just impeachment of his goodness, to display that grace "according to the pleasure of his own will."[9] Is it any act of injustice in Jehovah to punish sin? How then can God's decree make that arbitrary, which, without such a decree, is no more than just? If the actual condemnation of the sinner be righteous, the purpose of God to execute his righteous severity towards impenitent sinners cannot be lawfully arraigned.

In terms, therefore, the most decided, we disavow the charge of holding a doctrine, which, by necessary consequences, involves an arbitrary reprobation of any man irrespective of his crimes. And [we] are most fully persuaded that nothing can be more ungrateful or more unjust than to represent that as a cause of misery which is the alone source of all the mercy ever showed to man, or comfort enjoyed by him, in this world or in the next.

Second, the doctrine of sovereign distinguishing grace is represented as injurious to "the rich goodness, great mercy, and compassion of God to the sons of men." And the contrary doctrine, it is said, "tends more highly to the promotion of God's glory, because, the more there are benefited, the greater is the glory of the benefactor."

---

9 Ephesians 1:5.

But, brethren, let it be considered that no other doctrine save that of distinguishing grace secures the eternal benefit of a single individual of our race. For such is the deep depravity of the human heart that all the outward means of grace are of themselves totally ineffectual to man's everlasting salvation; insomuch, that after Christ himself had employed the best of external means with the Jews, he complains, "Ye will not come to me that ye might have life."[10] And upon this ground he asserts, "no man can come to me, except the Father who has sent me draw him."[11] Whence it follows that had not God sovereignly chosen some and resolved on their salvation, the death of Christ and the ministration of the gospel with all its appendages would have been in vain. So that the sovereign purpose and effectual operations of Jehovah, so far from diminishing his grace, tend highly to exalt it, since it is abundantly evident that there is more "grace, goodness, and compassion" manifested in securing the salvation of some, than in making ineffectual provision for the salvation of all.

Third, if the doctrine of distinguishing grace be true, we are told, "then the Jews could not be reasonably accused for not coming to Christ or not believing in him. Much less could it be imputed to them as their great crime that they would not come to him or believe in him."

Now that our Lord did accuse the Jews for not coming to him and believing in him, and that justly, we do not deny. But is there anything in the doctrine of salvation by grace which lessens the authority of the gospel or the obligations of men to embrace it? What more doth the gospel require of men than to believe what is true, to love what is good, to do what is right and to be sorry for what is wrong? And is it possible for any acts of divine mercy to make these obligations cease? If Christianity be properly attested,

---

10 John 5:40.
11 Cf. John 6:44.

ought it not to be believed? If God is good, ought he not to be loved? If the commandments of Christ are right, should they not be obeyed? And if he discovers to us our faults, ought we not to repent of them? All these in fact are natural duties arising from our necessary relation to the great God as our creator and moral governor, and it can never be demonstrated that God's special designs of grace to some annihilate the obligations of all the rest, any more than an earthly prince's discovering extraordinary regard to some of his subjects releases all his other subjects from their allegiance to him and subjection to the laws.

The obligations of men to believe the gospel arise from its being a divine revelation altogether worthy of God and sufficiently attested. And their obligations to obey the divine precepts are founded on their equity and their being enjoined by the authority of the moral governor of the world. So that unless it can be proved that God has no legal claim to the respect and obedience of any besides those whom he resolves to save and whose hearts he effectually inclines to keep his law, this objection has no force. And if it be admitted, it leaves every man who is not eventually saved at full liberty, without blame, to treat the blessed God of truth as a liar and tyrant! So that our doctrine by no means diminishes the guilt of man in rejecting the gospel, but allows us most cordially to unite with a celebrated writer of our own denomination, Dr. Gill, in asserting that a man "not coming to Christ, when revealed in the external ministry of the gospel as God's way of salvation, is criminal and blameworthy, since the disability and perverseness of his will are not owing to any decree in God, but to the corruption and vitiosity of his nature through sin. And, therefore, since his vitiosity of nature is blameworthy (for God made man upright), that which follows upon it, and is the effect of it, must be so too."[12]

---

12 John Gill, *The Cause of God and Truth* (London: Aaron Ward, 1735), I, 159–160 (the discussion of John 5:40).

Fourth, the doctrine of the sovereignty of divine mercy is charged with being "unfriendly to Christian activity, weakening the motives to diligence in religion, and thereby promoting the disuse of the means of grace."

We hope, brethren, that none of you by your conduct have put this objection into the mouths of your adversaries. If you have, the reproach be on you, not on the truth you profess. Do we not acknowledge the means as much a part of the divine plan as the end? And will not the same obligations lie against the providential government of God as are urged against the doctrine of sovereign salvation?

Let us inquire. Do you believe in a providence? Is that providence universal? And does it not secure the accomplishment of its immense designs? All this you allow; yet doth your confidence in a providence annihilate your industry? Are you husbandmen, and do you expect to reap where you have not sown? Are you merchants, and do you expect wealth without commerce? Are you artificers,[13] and do you expect to raise an edifice without labour? Is not the time of your life appointed,[14] but do you, on this account, neglect the use of medicine in sickness and food when in health? You attend to these as means necessary to the end. No less necessary do we consider the use of religious means in order to salvation. And from the very same motives and on the self-same principles on which you act in relation to the concerns of this life, do we conduct ourselves under the influence of our faith in the plans of grace, knowing that "what a man soweth that shall he also reap"[15] and "for all these things God will be sought unto by the house of Israel, to do it for them."[16]

Fifth, the doctrine of distinguishing grace is charged with "giving encouragement to careless sinners to presume groundlessly on

---

13 A skilled builder or craftsman.
14 See Job 14:5.
15 Galatians 6:7.
16 Cf. Ezekiel 36:37.

God's favour, and discouraging those who are willing to forsake sin from so doing, or cause them to despair of mercy."

But how can that doctrine encourage the careless sinner, which in terms the most decided declares the destruction of sin to be the ultimate object of God's designs? Is not the salvation to which we are chosen, represented by us as "through sanctification of the Spirit"[17]? And are not God's elect predestinated to conformity to the character of the Son of God, who was "holy, harmless, undefiled"[18]? And surely, to believe firmly that it is the design of God that his people "should be holy and without blame before him in love"[19] can have no tendency to "encourage careless sinners to presume on his favour."

That some hypocrites have abused the doctrine of grace, we admit; but what good thing exists which hath not been abused by wicked men? Thousands, from the forbearance of God, take encouragement fully to set their hearts in them to do evil. But doth their sin diminish the divine compassion? Do gluttony and drunkenness prove food to be poison? Or tyranny and despotism disprove the necessity or excellence of good government? Because there are some who turn the grace of God into lasciviousness, must the crime be imputed to the profession? Or shall those who are friendly to the doctrine of grace be charged with sinning that grace may abound? God forbid!

And what is there in this doctrine discouraging to a true penitent? Men that are careless about their salvation cannot be called penitents. Nor can they be discouraged from pursuing an object which they have no sincere desire to obtain. And as to those who are seeking the kingdom of God and his righteousness with their whole heart and with their whole soul, they are actually in possession of the fruits and evidences of God's distinguishing grace. And

17 2 Thessalonians 2:13.
18 Hebrews 7:26.
19 Ephesians 1:4.

can it discourage them to know that their holy desires and spiritual activity are beginnings of a saving work of God upon their hearts and that he always perfects what he begins? Is this discouraging? No, brethren, you and thousands more have derived encouragement and comfort from such views as these, which have "filled you with joy and peace in believing"[20] and put a new song into your mouths, even praise to the God of your salvation.[21]

Finally, it is urged that the doctrine of distinguishing grace is "injurious to personal religion, as it destroys all hope of obtaining salvation by our own performances."

To this we reply, first, this doctrine doth not constitute our performances worse in themselves, or less beneficial in their effects, but only takes for granted a certain truth, *viz.*, that our own righteousness is insufficient for our salvation. And therefore, unless it be injurious for a man to know the truth of himself respecting the depravity of his heart, this doctrine can never injure him.

Second, if personal religion can be no other ways promoted than by consideration of its meritorious influence, then we allow that our doctrine destroys it. But so far are we from imagining that real religion, such as the law requires and God approves, can be advanced by the hope of a deserved recompense, that we judge nothing can more effectively subvert it.

Real religion consists in supreme love to God and disinterested love to man. This is "not only the source and principle, but the very sum and substance, nay, the perfection of holiness." But service long and painful may be yielded for the hope of reward without any affection to the work or esteem for the employer, and therefore without any real religion. The tendency of any doctrine to promote personal piety is the same as its tendency to promote supreme love to God. And as all esteem rises from some real or supposed

---

20 Romans 15:13.
21 Cf. Psalm 40:3.

excellency in its object, whatever exhibits the great Jehovah in the true loveliness of his character must undoubtedly be calculated to improve our love for him. Now let it be considered with candour whether the doctrine we maintain doth not so represent the great Jehovah as most effectually to engage the admiration and esteem of every holy being in the universe.

The doctrine of distinguishing grace, when simplified, is summed up in three propositions:

1. All men have rebelled against God, and so rendered themselves obnoxious to his everlasting wrath.
2. It is the pleasure of God, for the sake of Jesus Christ, to extend a gracious pardon to a great number of his rebellious creatures and receive them into his favour as though they had never sinned.
3. God doth not extend his purpose of salvation to all, but while he saves some, leaves others exposed to the awful consequences of their crimes and the righteous awards of his most holy law.

This is a fair statement of the doctrine.

Let Jehovah then be viewed in his true character, "the judge of the whole earth."[22] And what measure could the supreme governor have pursued more becoming his name as the God of mercy and his character as the universal judge?

Justice, though an awful, is nevertheless a becoming and essential part of a judicial character, and therefore it is beautiful and lovely. Could we feel any esteem for the official character of a human minister of justice, who made a point of pardoning every criminal, let his crimes be as complicated or aggravated as they might? What licentiousness would he thereby introduce! What an encourager

---

22 Psalm 94:2.

would he be of vice and what an enemy to society! Of what advantage would be his tribunal and of what avail his office? Here we are persuaded that justice is essential to the loveliness of a legislator's character. And under whatever regulations his designs of mercy may be in his own breast, it is by threatening sin in general with punishment and by actually punishing a great number of transgressors he best maintains the respectability of his office and preserves order in that society of whose morals he is the guardian. For men will be most effectually deterred from evil by their knowing him to be a determined enemy to vice and seeing that none have any security but in their innocence. Whereas, if justice were never administered, every man would do what was right in his own eyes and the world [would] be filled with blasphemy, rebellion and every evil work.

Yet, as the legislator acts for the good of society wherever he perceives that clemency may be shown without endangering the public good, it will be an addition to his loveliness to display it. Especially if after a series of experiments it appear to the whole community that such acts of grace under the regulations of legislative wisdom have been to their advantage. They will then cheerfully leave the exercise of mercy to the discretion of their judge, and from experience persuaded that it will never be manifested to their injury, they will feel satisfaction and pleasure in every renewed instance of grace; and the disposition which the legislator shows to the exercise of clemency, whenever it is consistent with the honour of his government and the good of the community, will perfect their sentiments of his official beauty and loveliness.

Such, then, is the legislative beauty of Jehovah. He vindicates the honour of his government by permitting the law to take its course and thus shines in the glory of holiness. Yet mingling mercy with equity and forgiveness with justice "according to the counsel of his own will,"[23] every holy mind on a survey of his judicial

---

23 Ephesians 1:11.

character must exclaim, "He is the chief of ten thousand; he is altogether lovely."[24] Hence, the doctrines we avow, when rightly understood, are calculated to create and cherish that mixture of veneration and delight in our contemplation of the blessed God, wherein the essence of divine love and all true religion consist.

To this objection it may be answered, third: personal religion can never be injured by a right view of God's design in his gracious discriminations, because personal religion was the very thing for which he set apart his people, even "that they should be a peculiar people, zealous of good works."[25] Taught then by our Bibles that God chose us that we should be holy, we can no longer consider ourselves as possessed of the evidences of election, than whilst we enjoy in a measure the end of it. And hence we have a motive continually arising from the doctrine itself to "give all diligence to make our calling and election sure,"[26] being convinced that neither our believing the doctrine, nor expecting to be saved by it, are proofs of our security, any farther than attended with inward and personal religion.

Thus, brethren, have we endeavoured to assist you in maintaining "the faith once delivered to the saints."[27] We have only a few exhortations to annex in relation to this subject.

1. Whilst we wish you to be furnished with weapons of defence in case of an attack, we exhort you not to seek occasions of controversy with your fellow Christians. The religion of the heart generally declines as a controversial disposition prevails. It greatly injures the spirituality of the mind, and its effects everywhere demonstrate that those who indulge it are leaving the wheat for the chaff. To have Christians all of one mind is certainly, in some respects,

---

24 Song of Solomon 5:10, 16.
25 Titus 2:14.
26 2 Peter 1:10.
27 Jude 3.

highly desirable; but we must unite with the great Dr. Owen[28] in expecting that, should so delightful a period be ever known on this side heaven, the unanimity of Christians in sentiment will be the fruit of a previous spirit of love. And therefore, with affectionate ardour, we would urge upon you the excellent exhortations which were given by our venerable predecessors, the pastors of more than one hundred Baptist churches above a century ago. Having expressed their anxiety that whilst they defended the truth, they might carry themselves modestly and humbly towards those who differed from them, they add,

> And O that other contentions being laid asleep, the only care and contention of all upon whom the name of the blessed Redeemer is called, might for the future be to walk humbly with our God, and in the exercise of all love and meekness towards each other, to perfect holiness in the fear of the Lord, each one endeavouring to have his conversation such as becometh the gospel, and also suitable to his place and capacity, vigorously promoting in others the practice of true religion and undefiled in the sight of God our Father. And that in this backsliding day, we might not spend our breath in fruitless complaints of the evils of others, but may every one begin at home to reform in the first place our own hearts and ways, and then to quicken all that we may have influence upon to the same work; that if the will of God were so, none might deceive themselves by resting in, and trusting to, a form of godliness without the power of it, and inward experience of the efficacy of those truths that are professed by them.[29]

---

28 A reference to the Puritan theologian John Owen (1616–1683).

29 "To the Judicious and Impartial Reader," *The Baptist Confession of Faith* (Birmingham, Alabama: Solid Ground Christian Books/Carlisle, Pennsylvania: Reformed Baptist Publications, 2010), xiv–xv.

2. If you are called upon to defend the truth, see that it be done with meekness and prudence. If the former be wanting you will disgrace yourself; if the latter, the cause you espouse. "The professed friends of truth," says the eminent Dr. Witherspoon, "often injure the truth; they speak in such a manner as to confirm and harden enemies in their opposition to it. They use such incautious expressions as do indeed justify the objection, 'Shall we sin that grace may abound?' And in the heat of their zeal against the self-righteous legalist, seem to state themselves as enemies in every respect to the law of God, which is 'holy, just, and good'."[30] Remember, brethren, that it is impossible for God to injure his own government and set aside his own authority over his creatures. And therefore such modes of defending the truth as have any tendency to diminish the claims of Jehovah, or the obligations of men, must be unwarranted and indefensible.

3. Pray that your spirituality of mind, heavenly conversation and holiness of conduct may demonstrate to a gainsaying world that "the grace of God, which bringeth salvation," teacheth you habitually and decidedly to "deny ungodliness and evil works, and to live soberly, and righteously, and godly in the present evil world."[31] So shall you shine as lights on the earth, and by your good works will glory redound to your Father who is in heaven. To his paternal arms and heart we now commend you, resting in the fellowship of the gospel.

---

30 John Witherspoon, *Essay on the Connexion Between the Doctrine of Justification by the Imputed Righteousness of Christ and Holiness of Life* (2nd ed.; Edinburgh, 1756), 11–12 (Pearce has adapted the quote a little). This essay was reprinted numerous times in the nineteenth century as simply *An Essay on Justification*.
31 Titus 2:11–12.

*Baptist Missionary Society medallion*

*(from top left, William Carey, Andrew Fuller, Samuel Pearce, John Sutcliff and John Ryland, Jr.)*

# 21

## To William Carey[1]

London, August 27, 1795

My very dear brother,

...Be not discouraged, my dear brother, if you do not succeed immediately. You know the Brethren laboured nearly six years without effect in Greenland; but they persevered, and now a tenth part of the inhabitants of that country are professors of the faith of Christ.[2] But when I consider by what means they achieved so great a work, by the simple preaching of the cross of Christ and an exhibition of the love of his heart, I am constrained to say, "Not by might nor by power, but by thy Spirit, O Lord of Hosts."[3] I have lately been struck with a remark which applies to their labours and success. Facts interest more than speculations or abstract positions, however just. Talk to a child about any abstract subject and it requires pains to secure his attention; but tell him a story and he is

---

1 From *Missionary Correspondence*, 49–50.

2 A reference to one aspect of the missionary efforts of the Moravians, for whom Carey had deep admiration.

3 Zechariah 4:6. This verse was the motto of the Baptist Missionary Society.

all ear. So I should suppose an affectionate relation of the story of Jesus Christ, and his death and sufferings, would be the most likely way of engaging the heart of a heathen. But I, who am fifteen thousand miles from the seat of your labours, am almost ashamed to give my thoughts on a subject with which you must be so much better acquainted. Forgive my freedom and again believe me most affectionately yours in our dear Lord Jesus,

S. Pearce.

# 22

## *To William Carey*[1]

*Birmingham, August 12, 1796*

O my dear brother, did you but know with what feelings I resume my pen, freely to correspond with you after receiving your very affectionate letter to myself and perusing that which you sent by the same conveyance to the Society, I am sure you would persuade yourself that I have no common friendship for you and that your regards are at least returned with equal ardour.

I fear (I had almost said) that I shall never see your face in the flesh; but if anything can add to the joy which the presence of Christ and conformity, perfect conformity, to him will afford in heaven, surely the certain prospect of meeting with my dear brother Carey there is one of the greatest. Thrice happy should I be if the providence of God would open a way for my partaking of your labours, your sufferings and your pleasures, on this side the eternal world. But all my brethren here are of opinion that I shall be more useful at home than abroad; and I, though reluctantly,

---

1  From Fuller, *Memoirs of the Rev. Samuel Pearce*, 99–100, 102–104.

submit. Yet I am truly with you in Spirit. My heart is at Mudnabatty,[2] and at times I even hope to find my body there; but with the Lord I leave it. He knows my wishes, my motives, my regret. He knows all my soul; and, depraved as it is, I feel an inexpressible satisfaction that he does know it. However, it is a humbling thought to me that he sees I am unfit for such a station and unworthy of such an honour as to bear his name among the heathen. But I must be thankful still, that though he appoints me not to a post in foreign service, he will allow me to stand sentinel at home. In this situation may I have grace to be faithful unto death!...

With pleasure approaching to rapture, I read the last accounts you sent us. I never expected immediate success; the prospect is truly greater than my most sanguine hopes. "The kingdom of heaven is like to a little leaven hid in three measures of meal, till the whole is leavened."[3] Blessed be God! The leaven is in the meal, and its influence is already discoverable. A great God is doing great things by you.[4] Go on, my dearest brother, go on; God will do greater things than these. Jesus is worthy of a world of praise; and shall Hindustan not praise him? Surely he shall see of the travail of his soul there, and the sower and the reaper shall rejoice together. Already the empire of darkness totters, and soon it shall doubtless fall. Blessed be the labourers in this important work; and blessed be

---

2 Due to the fact that his financial reserves ran out soon after reaching India in 1793, Carey worked as the manager of an indigo factory at Mudnabati from 1794 to 1799. See S. Pearce Carey, *William Carey*, 160–189.

3 Cf. Matthew 13:33.

4 This statement is interesting in light of Carey's famous sermon on Isaiah 54:2–3, given at a meeting of the Northamptonshire Baptist Association in May 1792. The sermon encouraged Carey's fellow Baptists to trust God and venture forth to the nations with the message of the gospel, confident that God would bless that message and extend his kingdom. We do not know the details of the sermon that Carey preached, since no copy of the sermon exists. What we do know are the two main divisions of his message: "Let us expect great things. Let us attempt great things."

To William Carey

he who giveth them hearts and strength to labour and promises
that they shall not labour in vain!

Do not fear the want of money. God is for us, and the silver and
the gold are his; and so are the hearts of those who possess the most
of it. I will travel from the Land's End to the Orkneys, but we will
get money enough for all the demands of the Mission. I have never
had a fear on that head; a little exertion will do wonders, and past
experience justifies every confidence. Men we only want, and
God shall find them for us in due time. ...

I rejoice in contemplating a church of our Lord Jesus Christ in
Bengal, formed upon his own plan. Why do not the Hindu converts
join it? Lord, help their unbelief! But perhaps the drop is now
withheld that you may by and by have the shower, and lift up your
eyes and say, "These, whence came they? They fly as clouds, or as
doves to their windows."[5] For three years we read of few baptized
by the first disciples of our Lord; but, on the fourth, three thousand
and five thousand openly avowed him.[6] The Lord send you such
another Pentecost![7]

---

5  Cf. Isaiah 60:8.

6  See Acts 2:41 and 4:4.

7  Pearce's use of the term "Pentecost" here is similar to the way that a contemporary author would use the term "revival." For this use of the term "Pentecost" and
similar terms in the Reformed tradition, see Iain Murray, "Baptism with the Spirit:
What Is the Scriptural Meaning?" *The Banner of Truth*, 127 (April 1974): 5–22.

# 23

## To a young gentleman in Dublin[1]

### [1796]

Dear Master B—,

Your letter of the 21st of July gave me no small degree of pleasure, and should have been answered long before now, had not my numerous engagements at home compelled me to suspend my correspondence abroad. Except one letter, which I sent to Dublin to inform my friends of my safe return, this is the first day on which I have found time to write to Ireland since I left it. You will not, therefore, think me forgetful of you, or unconcerned about your prosperity. Believe me, from the first conversation that I had with you to the present moment, I have felt no small degree of solicitude for your eternal interests. Happy, indeed, shall I be to find that you continue anxious to secure them, for what are all the honours, the pleasures, or the wealth of this world, when compared with the spiritual and abiding blessings of religion? Could we insure all that

---

1 "Letter of the Late Mr. Pearce To a Young Gentleman in Dublin" in Rippon, ed., *Baptist Annual Register*, 3:498–499.

is esteemed by men, and enjoy it uninterruptedly for a thousand ages, yet, when those ages were past, how miserable should we be without religion? But life is short, and the pleasures of life are embittered by many crosses and trials, so that our earthly comforts yield but little good, "nor yield that little long."

It is, therefore, most blessed advice that our Saviour gives, John 6:27, "Labour not for the bread that perisheth, but for that bread which endureth in everlasting life," etc. Observe, my dear young friend, what our Saviour teaches you in these words. First, that religion is to the soul, what bread is to the body. It feeds, nourishes, and strengthens the mind. Secondly, this heavenly bread affords abiding comfort and support. It endures to everlasting life. Thirdly, the enjoyment of this sacred food deserves our most earnest pursuit. Labour for it. Let your whole heart and soul be in this great business of religion. If it be not fought and secured, how tremendous the consequences. The soul is lost, lost, lost, for—ever! Oh seek, therefore, my dear youth, "seek the Lord while he may be found, call upon him while he is near."[2] Draw nigh to him, and "he will draw near to you."[3] Fourthly, it must be received not as the reward of any good thing in you, or for any good thing to be done by you. The Son of man will give it to you. Yes, were we to have nothing but what we deserve, our best portion would be hell; but of his mercy he saveth us "according to his own purpose and grace, which was given us in Christ before the world began" (2 Timothy 1:9). From the mercy of Christ you must receive everything. Here you must apply for pardon. Here you must come for wisdom. Here you must seek strength and comfort—All is in "Christ, who of God is made unto us wisdom and righteousness, and sanctification and redemption" (1 Corinthians 1:30).

There is one thing, my dear Master B—, that you must not forget. Jesus Christ hath said it, and eternity shall prove it true, "Ye must

2  Isaiah 55:6.
3  James 4:8.

be born again,"[4] that is, your heart must be changed. It will not do that you are reformed, you must be renewed in the spirit of your mind. But this is a great thing, and what you can neither do yourself, nor can any creature do it for you; yet you must not be discouraged from seeking it, nor despair of obtaining it. Now, how is this great blessing to be obtained? Why, by following your dear father's advice "to pray often and from your heart." Yes, prayer is God's appointed means. "Ask," says he, "and you shall receive; seek, and ye shall find."[5] What can be more encouraging! You say, "You cannot pray as you wish to pray." I am glad to hear you say so; not that I rejoice in the imperfection of your prayers, but at your consciousness of their imperfections, and your sorrow on account of it. This, however, must comfort you, that God doth not answer our prayers for the sake of the goodness that is in them, but for the sake of his goodness, in whose name we pray. It is not for us to say, Is our prayer worthy? But we must say, Is Christ worthy? All God gives me, he gives for Christ's sake, and there is enough in one Christ for all his people, and as long as there is any virtue in his intercession, so long we may come with all boldness to a throne of grace, that we may obtain mercy and grace to help in time of need.

Having then boldness to enter into the holiest by the blood of Jesus, let us draw near in full assurance of faith,[6] and not give over wrestling with God till we obtain all the blessings which the blood of Jesus hath procured for sinners. But I have nearly filled my paper. Present my respects to your parents,...and do pray for, and soon write to, your very affectionate

S. Pearce.

---

4  John 3:7.
5  Cf. Matthew 7:7.
6  Cf. Hebrews 10:19,22.

# 24

## To William Summers[1]

### December 1796

I rejoice that you have been supported under and brought through your late trials. I do not wonder at it; for it is no more than God has promised. And though we may well wonder that he promises anything, yet his performance is no just ground of surprise; and when we find ourselves so employed, we had better turn our wonder to our own unbelief, that for one moment suspected God would not be as good as his word.

I have been lately more than ever delighted with the thought that God had engaged to do anything for such worms as we. I never studied the Deistical controversy so much,[2] nor ever rejoiced in

---

1 From Fuller, *Memoirs of the Rev. Samuel Pearce*, 115–116.

2 The controversy to which Pearce is referring was initiated by the publication of Thomas Paine's *The Age of Reason* in 1794 and 1795. Seeking to be better equipped to refute the anti–Christian philosophical perspectives of his day, Pearce had also spent a considerable amount of time reading the writings of the notorious Socinian Joseph Priestley (1733–1804), who, like Pearce, resided in Birmingham for a period of time. For a reference to Pearce's reading of Priestley, see Fuller, *Memoirs of the Rev. Samuel Pearce*, 191.

revelation more. Alas! What should we know if God had not con-
descended to teach us! Paul very justly remarks that no one knoweth
anything of God but the Spirit of God, and he to whom the Spirit
revealeth him.[3] Now the Spirit hath revealed God in the Bible; but
to an unbeliever the Bible is a sealed book. He can know nothing
from a book that he looks upon as an imposture, and yet there is
no other book in which God is revealed. So that to reject the Bible
is to immerse ourselves in darkness, and, whilst professing to be
wise, actually to become fools; whereas no sooner do we believe
what the Spirit saith, than unto us is God revealed and in his light
do we see light.[4]

---

3  See 1 Corinthians 2:10–11.
4  Cf. Psalm 36:9.

# 25

# *To John Ryland, Jr.*[1]

## *March 1797*

During the last three weeks I have, at times, been very poorly, with colds, etc. Am better now, and have been all along assisted in going through my public duties. Let us continue to pray for each other till death makes it a needless service. How uncertain is life, and what a blessing is death to a saint! I seem lately to feel a kind of affection for death. Methinks if it were visible I could embrace it.… To believe, to feel, to speak, to act exactly as God will have me; to be wholly absorbed and taken up with him; this, nothing short of this, can make my bliss complete. But all this is mine. Oh the height, the depth, the length, the breadth of redeeming love![2] It conquers my heart and constrains me to yield myself a living sacrifice, acceptable to God, through Jesus Christ. My dear brother, we have had many happy meetings on earth; the best is in reserve. …Oh how full of love and joy and praise

---

1  From Fuller, *Memoirs of the Rev. Samuel Pearce*, 116–117.

2  For the phrase, see Ephesians 3:18–19, where the same terms of measurement are given by the Apostle Paul, but in the exact reverse order.

shall we be when that happy state is ours! Well, yet a little while, and he that shall come will come. "Even so, come, Lord Jesus!"[3] My dear brother, forgive the hasty effusions of a heart that loves you in the bowels of Jesus and is always happy in testifying itself to be affectionately yours, S.P.

---

3  Revelation 22:20.

# 26

## *The Holy Scriptures*[1]

### *1797*

Reverence for divine revelation hath been in every period a discriminating characteristic of good men. In the early ages of the Jewish church, when, as yet, neither the devotional compositions of David, nor the sublime productions of succeeding prophets, had enriched the sacred page, "In those days the word of the Lord was precious."[2]

The royal Psalmist, not only possessed of the writings of Moses, but being also illuminated with the spirit of wisdom, and enraptured with the spirit of grace, exclaims, "O how I love thy law! It is my meditation day and night; I esteem thy statues above gold, yea more than fine gold; my soul breaketh for the longing it hath to thy judgements at all times; they are sweeter than honey or the

---

1 From *An Early Acquaintance with the Holy Scriptures Recommended* (Clipstone: J.W. Morris, 1800), 5–6, 8. This sermon on 2 Timothy 3:15 was originally preached in Abraham Booth's London meeting-house on August 13, 1797, for the Walworth Charity and Sunday-Schools for Poor Boys.

2 1 Samuel 3:1.

THE PIETY OF SAMUEL AND SARAH PEARCE

honey comb."[3] It is of these Scriptures that the apostle speaks in my text, as being known to Timothy from his early years, through the advantages of a pious education; for we find by the first chapter that his maternal ancestors for two generations were numbered with the faithful.[4]

...In our text [2 Timothy 3:15], and its connection, the apostle commends the Scriptures to our regard on three accounts:

1. The divinity of their origin, ver. 16: "They are given by the inspiration of God."
2. The purity of their nature, "The Holy Scriptures," which, like their divine author, are pure light and in them is no darkness at all.
3. Their beneficial tendency, "Able to make thee wise unto salvation."

It has indeed been questioned, whether the latter excellency attributed to the Scriptures be justly spoken of the writings of the Old Testament only, for if they were alone able to make us wise unto salvation, what necessity could there be for the additional books of the new? This is not a season for controversy. One remark only I would make: The apostle connects faith in Christ with a knowledge of the Old Testament—"through faith which is in Christ Jesus." Now that same faith into which Timothy was initi-ated, the New Testament exhibits to us; so that we must consider the assertion in the text as relating to the whole revelation of God. The Scriptures of both testaments contain truths which instruct us in the way of salvation.

How great the encomium![5] Here this sacred volume stands

---

3 Psalm 119:97,127,20; 19:10. Pearce is quoting from the King James Version, but he has made some slight changes to the wording.

4 See 2 Timothy 1:5.

5 Meaning the praise or glory of it.

unrivalled. Some books may instruct us how to obtain wealth, others may assist us in maintaining or restoring health, and others may make us wise to secure a reputation; but the Bible alone can make us wise to salvation.

That man is a sinner and that his sin diminishes his present enjoyment and endangers all his future happiness, every conscience witnesses; but whom did the light of nature ever instruct in the way of salvation? Not to appeal to the ignorant Otaheitan, nor to the uncivilized Hottentot,[6] let the interesting inquiry, "What must I do to be saved?" be put to the civilized, the enlightened heathen, to a Tully[7] or a Socrates, what reply could they have given? Or, to a mind conscious of its depravity, burdened with guilt, tortured with fearful apprehension of almighty indignation, and panting to know whether its crimes might be forgiven, what peace could they have administered? It is probable they might conjecture the fact, but what truly awakened sinner can rest his hopes on a basis so precarious?

But from Revelation, from the Holy Scriptures, we obtain the amplest satisfaction on this important subject. Here mercy, heavenly mercy, appears with pardons in her hands. Here the God we have offended passeth by us, proclaiming his name, "The Lord God, gracious and merciful, slow to anger, pardoning iniquity, transgression and sin."[8] Here we see a thousand sinners like ourselves successfully pleading for forgiveness, or rejoicing in the mercy they have found. "I acknowledged unto thee," saith one, "my transgression, and thou forgaveth the iniquity of my sin. I sought the Lord, and he heard me, and delivered me from all my fears. Come ye that

---

6 An Otaheitan was a native Tahitian. Tahiti was called Otaheite in the eighteenth century. Hottentot was the eighteenth-century European name for the Khoikhoi or Khoi of southern Africa.

7 Tully was the Anglicization of the *nomen* of the Roman orator and philosopher Marcus Tullius Cicero (106–43 B.C.).

8 See Exodus 34:6.

fear God, and I will tell you what he hath done for my soul."[9]
Says another, "Behold, for peace I had great bitterness; but thou in
love to my soul hast cast all my sins behind thy back."[10] Whilst a
third, penetrated with humility, and glowing with gratitude,
exclaims, "I was a blasphemer, and a persecutor, and injurious; but
I obtained mercy!"[11]

In these sacred pages too we find the God of mercy kindly
inviting us, guilty as we are, to "come boldly to a throne of grace,
that we may receive mercy, and obtain grace to help in time of
need."[12] Here also the curtain that hides the world of glory from
our view is drawn aside; and in heaven we see an innumerable
company of happy saints, once sinners as we are today, but made
perfect now both in purity and bliss, celebrating the mercy of God
in everlasting hymns.

And do the Scriptures bring all this to view? Do they lay a
foundation on which one so vile as I may securely build my hope
of reconciliation to my God? Blessed volume! I receive thee as
the shepherds received the descending angels who brought the
glad tiding of a Saviour for all people: I receive thee "with fear
and great joy."[13]

Nor is this all; my heart asks another question: "How is this salvation to be obtained?" And the Holy Scriptures afford me all the
satisfaction that I desire: they not only point out the object, but also
put me in the road, and furnish me with supplies all the way, whilst
I am "pressing towards the mark for the prize of my high calling."[14]
"I am the way," said Jesus the Son of God; "no man cometh unto

---

9 See Psalm 32:5; 34:4; and 66:16.
10 Isaiah 38:17.
11 1 Timothy 1:13.
12 Hebrews 4:16.
13 This phrase is taken from Matthew 28:8.
14 See Philippians 3:14.

the Father but by me."[15] And in perfect union with the declarations of the master, are those of his inspired servants. "This (they assure me) is a faithful saying, and worthy of all acceptation, that Jesus Christ came into the world to save sinners"[16]; that there is "a new and living way consecrated through the veil, that is to say, his flesh"[17]; that "he died for our offences, and rose again for our justification"[18]; and "is now exalted to be a Prince and a Saviour, to give repentance unto Israel and remission of sins"[19]; and that "having suffered, the just for the unjust, to bring us to God,"[20] "God is just and yet the justifier of the ungodly."[21]

Do I enquire farther, how I am to enjoy a sensible participation of the blessings of salvation? The Holy Scriptures say, "He that believeth on the Son hath everlasting life."[22] They teach me that whoever truly and heartily receives the Lord Jesus as exhibited in the gospel, as his infallible teacher, his atoning priest, and rightful sovereign so as to believe his doctrine, rely on his mediation and delight in obedience to his laws, shall be saved. And that no sincere enquirer may be at a loss to judge whether he be personally interested in this salvation or not, the Holy Scriptures declare that such a dedication of the soul to God being accomplished through his gracious influence upon the heart will be attended with such an effectual, universal, and abiding change in the feelings, temper and conduct, that such an one will be, as it were, "a new creature"[23]; that he will henceforth take delight in prayer, and other exercises of religion, mourn over his sins before God, be kind and affectionate

---

15 John 14:6.
16 1 Timothy 1:15.
17 Hebrews 10:20.
18 Romans 4:25.
19 Acts 5:31.
20 1 Peter 3:18.
21 Romans 3:26.
22 John 3:36.
23 2 Corinthians 5:17.

to his enemies, prefer the society of the Lord's people to that of all other men, and be looking with cheerful expectation for that "blessed hope, and the glorious appearing of the great God, and our Saviour, Jesus Christ."[24]

Finally, to encourage every humble follower of the Lamb, this sacred volume promises support under every trial and in every duty; preservation by the divine power whilst on earth; and to crown all at last, the felicity of heaven, consisting in the everlasting deliverance of the soul from ignorance, guilt, misery and sin, and the body from pain, disease, corruption and death, all of which shall be enjoyed in the society of holy angels, the whole company of the redeemed, and the Lord Jesus himself, in whose "presence there is fulness of joy, and at whose right hand there are pleasures for evermore."[25]

24 Titus 2:13.
25 See Psalm 16:11.

# 27

# *To John Ryland, Jr.*[1]

*Birmingham, October 8, 1798*

O my dear brother, your letter of the 5th which I received this morning has made me thankful for all my pulpit agonies; as they enable me to weep with a weeping brother. They have been of use to me in other respects, particularly in teaching me the importance of attaining and maintaining that spirituality and pious ardour in which I have found the most effectual relief, so that on the whole I must try to "glory in tribulations also."[2] I trust I often can after the conflict is past, but to glory "in" them, especially in mental distresses—*hic labor, hoc opus est.*[3]

But how often has it been found that when ministers have felt themselves most embarrassed, the most effectual good has been done to the people. O for hearts entirely resigned to all the will of God!

---

1 Ms. John Ryland RG no.1126, The American Baptist Historical Society Archives (Atlanta, Georgia). Used with permission. A portion of the letter is also found in Fuller, *Memoirs of the Rev. Samuel Pearce*, 130–131.

2 Cf. 2 Corinthians 12:9.

3 Latin, "this toil, this is [my] work."

How happy should I be could I always enjoy the sympathies of a brother who is tried in these points as I of late have often been! Were Bristol[4] a village instead of a city and a congregation less gay[5] and smaller than my own to desire my service I confess the thought of being near to you would almost incline me to wish an open door for my removal. As things are I must thankfully endeavour to improve my present station and pray that the great head of the Church would be pleased in giving the people at Broadmead another teacher after his own heart to give you a friend and brother after yours....

Cooper from London is here.[6] I heard part of a sermon last night from him, after our service was over, which I should have very much liked if the fly of Egotism had not spoiled the ointment, e.g. "*I* have found that *my* preaching has been blessed when *I* etc." Had he an affectionate and judicious friend at hand... [I] should hope he has materials for a valuable minister in the Church of God. O what a lovely garment is humility! May the Lord clothe with it from head to foot.

Your unworthy but affectionate brother,

S. Pearce.

---

4  Ryland was serving in Bristol.

5  That is, less brilliant or less fine.

6  There were a few men by the name of "Cooper" who were preaching in Baptist circles at this time, and further identification has not been possible.

# 28

## To Matthew Griffith[1]

### Birmingham, November 13, 1798

My dear M.

I can only confess my regret at not replying to yours at a much earlier period, and assure you that the delay has been accidental,

---

1 From Fuller, *Memoirs of the Rev. Samuel Pearce*, 132–135. For the identification of Matthew Griffith as the recipient of this letter, see Andrew Fuller, *Memoirs of the Rev. Samuel Pearce*, 138. Matthew Griffith, a Baptist from Worcester, had asked Pearce's advice about how to prepare for studies at Bristol Baptist Academy. Griffith went to the Academy, but his conduct there was far from being above reproach. He ended up being asked to leave the college for having engaged in "antenuptial fornication" (prenuptial sex). John Newton (1725–1807), who was actually the means of introducing Griffith to Pearce, wrote to Ryland that he was deeply distressed by Griffith's conduct: "his conduct has hurt me much, because I loved him much, I shall mourn and pray for him in secret. The Lord grant that he may be humbled by what is past, and get strength, by the proof of his own weakness. I mean, may the Lord pardon him, and lead him to a more simple dependence upon himself who alone is able to keep us from falling, or to raise us when we are down" (John Newton, Letter to John Ryland, Jr., May 28, 1801, Bristol Baptist College Archives, Bristol). On Matthew Griffith, see Grant Gordon, ed., *Wise Counsel: John Newton's Letters to John Ryland, Jr.* (Edinburgh/Carlisle, Pennsylvania: The Banner of Truth Trust, 2009), 347, 350–351, 390–391, 393.

and not designed. I felt the importance of your request for advice. I was sensible it deserved some consideration before it was answered. I was full of business at the moment. I put it by, and it was forgotten; and now it is too late. The time of your going to Bristol draws nigh. If, instead of an opinion respecting the best way of occupying your time before you go, you will accept a little counsel during your continuance there, I shall be happy at any time to contribute such a mite as my experience and observation have put in my power.

At present, the following rules appear of so much moment, that, were I to resume a place in any literary establishment, I would religiously adopt them as the standard of my conduct.

First, I would cultivate a spirit of habitual devotion. Warm piety connected with my studies, especially at my entrance upon them, would not only assist me in forming a judgement on their respective importance, and secure the blessing of God upon them; but would so cement the religious feeling with the literary pursuit, as that it might abide with me for life. The habit of uniting these, being once formed, would, I hope, be never lost. And I am sure that, without this, I shall both pursue trivial and unworthy objects, and those that are worthy I shall pursue for a wrong end.

Secondly, I would determine on a uniform submission to the instructions of my preceptor, and study those things which would give him pleasure. If he be not wiser than I am, for what purpose do I come under his care? I accepted the pecuniary help of the Society on condition of conforming to its will, and it is the Society's will that my tutor should govern me.[2] My example will have influence: let me not, by a single act of disobedience, or by a word that

---

2 This is a reference to the Bristol Education Society that had been formed in 1770 by Hugh Evans (1713–1781) and his son Caleb Evans, who had been Principal of the Bristol Baptist Academy when Pearce had been there. This Society provided financial support for potential ministers. Griffith received financial support for his board and tuition from Christmas 1799 to the middle of the summer of 1800.

implicates dissatisfaction, sow the seeds of discord in the bosoms of my companions.

Thirdly, I would pray and strive for the power of self–government, to form no plan, to utter not a word, to take no step, under the mere influence of passion. Let my judgement be often asked, and let me always give it time to answer. Let me always guard against a light or trifling spirit; and particularly as I shall be amongst a number of youths whose years will incline them all to the same frailty.

Fourthly, I would in all my weekly and daily pursuits observe the strictest order. Always let me act by a plan. Let every hour have its proper pursuit; from which let nothing but a settled conviction that I can employ it to better advantage ever cause me to deviate. Let me have fixed time for prayer, meditation, reading, languages, correspondence, recreation, sleep, etc.

Fifthly, I would not only assign to every hour its proper pursuit; but what I did I would try to do with all my might. The hours at such a place are precious beyond conception, till the student enters on life's busy scenes. Let me set the best of my class ever before me, and strive to be better than they. In humility and diligence, let me aim to be the first.

Sixthly, I would particularly avoid a versatile habit. In all things I would persevere. Without this, I may be a gaudy butterfly; but never, like the bee, will my hive bear examining. Whatever I take in hand, let me first be sure I understand it, then duly consider it, and, if it be good, let me adopt and use it.

To these, my dear brother, let me add three or four things more minute, but which, I am persuaded, will help you much. Guard against a large acquaintance while you are a student. Bristol friendship, while you sustain that character, will prove a vile thief, and rob you of many an invaluable hour. Get two or three of the students, whose piety you most approve, to meet for one hour in a week for experimental conversation and mutual prayer. I found this highly beneficial, though, strange to tell, by some we were persecuted for our practice! Keep a diary.[3] Once a week at furthest, call yourself to an account. What advances you have made in your different studies, in divinity, history, language, natural philosophy, style, arrangement; and, amidst all, do not forget to inquire, "Am I more fit to serve and to enjoy God than I was last week?"

---

3   Eighteenth-century Baptists like Pearce inherited diary-keeping as a spiritual discipline from their Puritan forebears. John Sutcliff, for example, encouraged William Carey to keep "two journals" to record his walk with God. Carey admitted the wisdom of the advice, but told Sutcliff that "owing to my numerous avocations, which engross all my time, I have long since dropped the practice of keeping any journal at all." See William Carey, Letter to John Sutcliff, January 16, 1798, in Eustace Carey, *Memoir of William Carey, D.D.* (London: Jackson and Walford, 1836), 322.

# 29

## To the Lascars[1]

*Late autumn 1798*

Lascars!

You are far from home, and in a country of strangers. Most of the Europeans you have been accustomed to observe, have perhaps discovered a desire for nothing but gain, or honour, or personal indulgence. But you know not all. In this strange land there are many who think of you, weep over you, and pray to the great Allah for you.[2] Their hearts are filled with the most affectionate concern for your happiness. Some have observed, and others have inquired after your manner of life. And they are grieved to find that your bodies, and the pursuits of this world, engage all your attention. They

---

1 "Letter to the Lascars" in Rippon, ed., *Baptist Annual Register*, 3:433–438. A Lascar was an Indian or Southeast Asian sailor. The word is a loanword from a Persian and Urdu word *laškarī*, meaning "soldier." Pearce wrote this excellent example of an eighteenth-century evangelical tract in the late autumn of 1798. See Payne, *First Generation*, 50.

2 Pearce here uses the term "Allah" as a term for God. Many evangelicals today would strongly disagree with such usage.

consider that you have immortal souls within you, and they send you this paper to beseech you to consider it with seriousness. Consider that this life is the passage to another, and that while you are unconcerned about eternity, you cannot be prepared for it. You profess to believe that there is a God, who made you and all things. God has not made all things alike. Some creatures have no capacity for attaining the knowledge of God, as the beasts, birds and fishes. And as they cannot know God nor his will, so there is no good nor evil in their doings. But you, who are made capable of this great attainment, you, who must live forever, are accountable for all your actions. God hears everything you say, and sees everything you do. God knows all your thoughts, and desires, and purposes; and he will call you to an account for all at the great Day when he shall judge the world in righteousness.

Were you ever concerned to know what you must do to please God? Did you ever consider that, as he gives you your life and all its comforts, you ought therefore to praise him? That, as you are constantly dependent upon him for all things, you ought to pray to him; and that as he is altogether good and holy, you ought supremely to love him and delight in him. Surely, if you have never thought upon these things before, it is now high time to begin, lest you should die in your sins, and God at last should say, concerning each of you, "Here is a vile ungrateful Lascar, whom I made, and fed, and clothed, and preserved all the days of his life; but he never thought upon me, never praised me, never loved me. Cast him into hell forever!"

You believe that Moses was a prophet. By him God gave his law to man in writing. That law requires all men to love God with all their heart, and to love their neighbour as they love themselves. No law could be more just than this; for God is infinitely good himself and is the author of all the good in the universe. And as to men, we are all descended from one father, and therefore we all ought to love one another as brethren. Nor could any law be given, the observance of which, would so effectually benefit ourselves; for if we love God supremely, and one another disinterestedly, we shall all be peaceful and happy, since all the misery that exists in the world is owing to nothing else but a want of love to God and one another. And, indeed, God himself denounces the most awful vengeance on every soul that doeth man evil, and breaketh his most good and holy law; for by the same prophet, Moses, he has declared, "Cursed is everyone who continueth not in all things written in the book of the law to do them."[3]

Alas! alas! All men have broken this good law. We have broken it; you have broken it; and therefore we are all sinners under the curse of God. And, oh! what a dreadful thing it is for a rational, immortal being to be cursed by the blessed God, and cursed forever.

What then will you do to be saved? How will you escape the damnation of hell? Can you pay the debt you have contracted? Can you blot out the remembrance of your sins from the mind of God? Can you evade his search, flee from his vengeance, induce a change in his purposes, or defy his power? As well might you attempt to drain the ocean or displace the stars.

What then will you do? O, dear Lascars! we send you glad tidings of great joy. The God whom we have offended, hath taken pity on us, and in his love and mercy, has raised up an all-sufficient Saviour: a Saviour fit for us, and fit for you; able to save us both to the uttermost[4]; to restore us to the enjoyment of God, from whom we have wandered, to fill us with a sense of his love in life, to comfort us when we are sinking in death, and to raise us to the enjoyment of immortal blessedness.

In communicating these glad tidings to you, we do not deceive you with the words of man's invention. We have the authority of the great God himself for what we say, and the experience of our

---

3  Galatians 3:10, referring to Deuteronomy 27:26.
4  See Hebrews 7:25.

own hearts assures us of its truth. Once indeed we were all like you, ignorant of our guilty and dangerous state. We thought only about being happy in this world. But the more we strove to be so, the more wretched we became. Till at length, it pleased God to teach us the danger of dying as we were, and the folly of delaying, for a single moment, to search if salvation might be obtained. Our hearts were filled with fear, and we put the same question to ourselves which we have now put to you. What must we do to be saved? Then we fell down before God, and confessed that we were rebellious sinners, who had deserved his everlasting anger; and that, if he punished us forever, he would do us no wrong. We earnestly entreated him for his mercy, and besought him to show to us some way of salvation. Behold he was graciously entreated of us. He sent his word, and healed us.[5] He made known to us the way of peace; and, dispelling fear from our hearts, filled them with consolation and joy.

Now, no sooner did we taste these inestimable blessings, than, such was their nature, they begot in us the most earnest longings that every poor sinner in the world might be made as happy as ourselves.

We saw the world lying in wickedness, the far greater part of mankind living like brutes, thoughtless of themselves and God. Among these, dear Lascars, we beheld you. God, who had mercy on us, moved us to pity your unhappy state, and in sincere affection to tell you the way to be happy here, and forever.

Hear, then Lascars! the heavenly message. "God so loved the world, that he gave his only begotten Son, that whosoever believeth in him might not perish, but have everlasting life."[6] The great Gift of God to us, and for us, is Jesus Christ. You perhaps have been taught that this Jesus was only a prophet, like Moses, and could do

---

5  Cf. Psalm 107:20.
6  John 3:16.

no more for you. But you have been misled. The Jewish prophets who came before him most plainly foretold that he was to be a divine Saviour; and his disciples, who were taught from his own lips, went about the world, declaring that they had found him of whom Moses in the law and the prophets had written, even Jesus of Nazareth, who they affirmed, as to his natural descent, came from the stock of Abraham, but who was also "God over all, blessed forever."[7] And all who heartily received their report, found, as we also have, deliverance, and peace, and joy, by believing on his name.

You allow that Jesus was God's prophet. Now he said that he and the Father were one,[8] so that they who honoured the Son did honour the Father also.[9] But the prophets of God do not lie, and therefore we adore him as the Son of God.

This blessed Saviour, for the great love that he bore to us poor sinners, from before the foundation of the world, at length clothed himself in our nature, and became bone of our bone and flesh of our flesh.[10] For he was born of a virgin, in whose womb he was formed by the power of God, on which account he was free from all sin in his nature. And when he grew up to manhood, although many who were his enemies, because he preached so faithfully against their wicked practices, continually watched him to find some evil, of which they might accuse him, yet they could find none. For the first thirty years of his life, he lived mostly in obscurity, but at length he made a more public appearance. Twice did the Holy Father give notice of his dignity, by proclaiming from heaven, "This is my beloved Son, in whom I am well pleased, hear ye him."[11] Then he went forth in his omnipotent goodness. He raised men to life from death and the grave, and daily employed himself in healing

---

7  Cf. Romans 9:5.

8  John 10:30.

9  See John 5:23.

10 See Genesis 2:23.

11 See Luke 3:22 and 9:35, and parallels in the gospels of Matthew and Mark.

all manner of sickness and diseases among the people, without a single failure. This he did in the sight of all ranks of men, for three years together. And when the fame of his miracles drew the people around him, his heart being filled with compassion and tender love to them he faithfully told them of their sins, seriously warned them of their danger, exhorted them to repent and affectionately invited them to come to him for salvation, promising them the remission of their sins, and the gift of everlasting life.

But the remission of our sins cost him most grievous sufferings, for nothing besides his precious blood was sufficient for our redemption. Yet so much was his heart set upon our salvation, that he was content to undergo the severest torments, and to die the most shameful and cruel death, rather than we should be lost forever.

This, Lascars, this is the blessed news! These are the glad tidings of great joy which must be preached to all people, and which the God of heaven, by our means, now sends to you. Jesus was crucified for us. He died that we may live. He suffered that we may be happy.

Behold, here, the mystery of his incarnation and learn why God was manifested in the flesh.[12] Had he not put on our nature, how could he have suffered in our place? And if he had not been divine, of what more value would his blood have been then the blood of one of us, or one of you?

But now we cannot doubt of the efficacy of his sufferings, who was at once the Son of God and the Son of Man. And who can but admire and adore the grace of our Lord Jesus Christ, that he should endure such agonies for us?

Jesus shed his blood for the Jews, and there were thousands of the posterity of Abraham, who believed in his name, and loved him till they died. Jesus died for Gentiles too. He died for us, and since we knew his love, our hearts have been drawn to love him in return.

---

12 See 1 Timothy 3:16.

Jesus died for Lascars! Jesus suffered unnumbered tortures for Lascars! O Lascars, have you no love to Jesus? Long indeed you have remained ignorant of our dear Saviour; but now God has made sailors of you, and sent you to England, that you might no longer be unacquainted with Jesus. O, how great the privilege that you hear his blessed name, and are taught the truths of his great salvation before you die. Lascars! receive into your hearts this word of life. Give thanks to God that you are not suffered to perish for want of a Saviour. Put your trust in the Almighty Jesus, and yield yourselves to him as living sacrifices. Then shall you have the witness in yourselves that he is the Son of God, for you will find such peace, such joy, such delight in God, such desires after purity, such love to our Saviour and to all who love him too, of every country and of every colour, as will assure your hearts more strongly than all the force of arguments that the religion of Jesus came from heaven, and that it leads thither every soul who sincerely embraces it.

Consider, dear Lascars! this Jesus, though he died, yet he arose again to life on the third day, after which he ascended up into heaven, to dwell with his Father, and to govern the world, until he shall come the second time to judge all men, and fix their states for ever, when it will be found that those who have believed on him, and owned him before men, shall be eternally saved, but those who persist in disbelieving on his name, shall be everlastingly condemned.

Lascars! believe in the Lord Jesus Christ, and ye shall be saved!

# 30

## *To William Carey*[1]

*Birmingham, March 1799*

Dear, very dear brother,

The last letter that I wrote you, though dated in September, was not finished till the beginning of October, when I promised, unless anything extraordinary should occur, that I would write you a letter regularly every month from that time. It is now March 1799 and I have not yet written. Is it because I have ceased to love you? No, my dear brother! I must first lose all my recollection, my reason, and my virtue.

The fact is that on my return from the last Kettering Mission meeting I took a violent cold, which, being neglected, got worse.[2] And, thinking that pulpit sweats would effect a cure, I remitted none of my labours either at home or among the villages; on the contrary, after walking several miles, I sometimes preached an extra sermon. This was imprudent. My lungs became inflamed and at length were

---

1  From *Missionary Correspondence*, 71
2  See pages 38–41.

so exceedingly irritable that I could not even converse in private for two minutes without pain and danger. The doctor ordered me to keep myself undisturbed and unemployed, saying that if it were the end of March instead of November he could give me better hopes of recovery, for he thought that either a warmer climate or a warmer season was absolutely necessary.

Do you think, my dear brother, that when the doctor mentioned a warmer climate I was without thoughts of Mudnabatty. Ah, thought I, had the Society sent me there when I so earnestly entreated them, I had not now been shut out from all service for God and enjoyment of his people for want of a warmer climate. For some time a discharge of blood, a pain in my side, a loss of appetite, soreness in my breast and an irregular pulse, led me to apprehend that death was fast approaching. Sweet were the thoughts of dying. And although I could not but regret that I should leave this world without having made one effort for the salvation of the "sinners of the Gentiles" personally among them, yet that I had indirectly at least endeavoured the accomplishment of that most desirable object was a matter of inexpressible satisfaction and delight.

I greatly accused myself of inactivity in the Redeemer's cause. I saw that my zeal had been tardy, unequal, and perhaps often ineffectual, for want of being more ardent and persevering. Yet the thought that the Lord had ever employed me, that I had not been quite idle, that some good had been done, some portions of divine truth propagated, some daring sinners reclaimed, some broken hearts bound up and comforted, some additions made to the Church of the Lord Christ, and some improvement in knowledge, devotion, and virtue, among his people: these were occasions of grateful delight. So that, with all my numberless infirmities and crimes, I was enabled to say, I have not lived nor run in vain. ...

Yours very affectionately,

S. Pearce

# 31

## To Andrew Fuller[1]

### Plymouth, April 18, 1799

The last time that I wrote to you was at the close of a letter sent to you by brother Ryland. I did not like that postscript form; it looked so card-like as to make me fear that you would deem it unbrotherly. After all, perhaps, you thought nothing about it; and my anxieties might arise only from my weakness, which seems to be constantly increasing my sensibilities. If ever I felt love in its tenderness for my friends, it has been since my affliction. This, in a great measure, is not more than the love of "publicans and harlots, who love those that love them."[2] I never conceived myself by a hundred degrees so interested in the regards of my friends as this season of affliction has manifested I was; and therefore, so far from claiming any "reward" for loving them in return, I should account myself a monster of ingratitude were it otherwise. Yet there is something in affliction itself, which, by increasing the delicacy of our feelings

---

1  From Fuller, *Memoirs of the Rev. Samuel Pearce*, 144–147.
2  Cf. Matthew 21:32 and 5:46.

and detaching our thoughts from the usual round of objects which present themselves to the mind when in a state of health, may be easily conceived to make us susceptible of stronger and more permanent impressions of an affectionate nature.

I heard at Bristol that you and your friends had remembered me in your prayers at Kettering. Whether the Lord whom we serve may see fit to answer your petitions on my account or not, may they at least be returned into your own bosoms.

For the sake of others I should be happy could I assure you that my health was improving. As to myself, I thank God that I am not without "a desire to depart and to be with Christ, which is far better."[3] I find that neither in sickness, nor in health, I can be so much as I wish like him whom I love. "To die is gain"[4]; oh to gain that state, those feelings, that character, which perfectly accord with the mind of Christ and are attended with the full persuasion of his complete and everlasting approbation! I want no heaven but this; and to gain this, most gladly would I this moment expire. But if to abide in the flesh be more needful for an individual of my fellow men,[5] Lord, let thy will be done; only let Christ be magnified by me, whether in life or death![6]

The weather has been so wet and windy since I have been at Plymouth that I could not reasonably expect to be much better; and I cannot say that I am much worse. All the future is uncertain. Professional men[7] encourage me; but frequent returns appear and occasional discharges of blood check my expectations. If I speak but for two minutes, my breast feels as sore as though it were scraped with a rough-edged razor; so that I am mute all the daylong and have actually learned to converse with my sister by means of our fingers....

---

3  Philippians 1:23.
4  Philippians 1:21.
5  Cf. Philippians 1:24.
6  See Philippians 1:20.
7  That is, physicians.

*Andrew Fuller (1754–1815)*

Unless the Lord work a miracle for me, I am sure that I shall not be able to attend the Olney meeting.[8] It is to my feelings a severe anticipation; but how can I be a Christian and not submit to God?

---

8  This meeting on May 7 saw the commissioning of William Ward, Daniel Brunsdon (d.1801) and his wife as missionaries for India at Olney, where Sutcliff was the pastor. A similar meeting, for Joshua (1768–1837) and Hannah Marshman (1767–1847) and William Grant (d.1799) and his wife, had taken place at Bristol four days earlier. Pearce wrote a letter to Fuller to be read at the May 7 meeting. See pages 189–191.

# 32

## *To John Ryland, Jr.*[1]

*Plymouth, April 14, 1799*

Very dear brother,

My health is in much the same state as when I wrote last, excepting that my muscular strength rather increases and my powers of speaking seem less and less every week. I have for the most part spoken only in whispers for several days past; and even these seem too much for my irritable lungs. My father asked me a question today. He did not understand me when I whispered; so I was obliged to utter one word, and one word only, a little louder and that brought on a soreness, which I expect to feel till bedtime.

I am still looking out for fine weather; all here is cold and rainy. We have had but two or three fair and warm days since I have been here; then I felt better. I am perfectly at a loss even to guess what the Lord means to do with me; but I desire to commit my ways to him and be at peace. I am going today about five miles into the country to Tamerton, where I shall await the will of God concerning me....

---

1  From Fuller, *Memoirs of the Rev. Samuel Pearce*, 148–149.

My dear brother, I hope you will correspond much with Kettering.[2] I used to be a medium; but God has put me out of the way. I could weep that I can serve him no more; and yet I fear some would be tears of pride. Oh for perfect likeness to my humble Lord!

---

2  An encouragement to Ryland to maintain a regular correspondence with Fuller. Ryland really needed no such encouragement, since he and Fuller were extremely close friends. See Michael A.G. Haykin, "On Friendship," *Reformation Today*, 140 (July-Aug 1994): 26–30.

# 33

## To Andrew Fuller[1]

*Tamerton [Devon], May 2, 1799*

I am so weak that close thinking and writing excite or increase my feverish sensations; yet, I would gladly offer a few hints to the Society and to the Missionaries. Only three things have particularly struck me. You and others will probably think of more.

First, as this Society is dependent for its support on the pious public, whose least compensation should be an acquaintance with the success of those for whom their benevolence is exerted, it is highly proper that each missionary under the patronage of this Society should communicate direct and personal information concerning his own efforts, and their various fruits, at least twice in

---

1 From *Periodical Accounts Relative to the Baptist Missionary Society* (Clipstone: J.W. Morris, 1800), I, 516–519. Pearce wrote this letter to be read at the May 7 commissioning of William Ward and the Brunsdons for service in India (see page 185, note 8). When Ward wrote to Pearce to tell him about this meeting, he said that this letter from Pearce "produced a flood of tears" among those assembled (Letter from William Ward, May 13, 1799, cited "Biographical Notices: The Rev. Samuel Pearce" in John Taylor, *Biographies. Northamptonshire* (Northampton: Taylor & Son, 1901), 11. This letter from Ward also gives a description of this meeting at Olney.

every year; to which end the Society do request that each of their missionaries would keep a regular journal of his proceedings and send it, or a copy of it, to the secretary by the spring and fall ships.

Secondly, since that kingdom which we as the disciples of Jesus wish to establish is not of this world, we affectionately and seriously enjoin on each missionary under our patronage that he do cautiously and constantly abstain from every interference with the political concerns of the country where he may be called to labour, whether by words or deeds; that he be obedient to the laws in all civil affairs; that he respect magistrates, supreme and subordinates; and teach the same things to others. In fine, that he apply himself wholly to the all-important concerns of that evangelical service to which he has so solemnly dedicated himself.

Thirdly, however gross may be the idolatries and heathenish superstitions that may fall beneath a missionary's notice, the Society are nevertheless persuaded that both the mutual respect due from man to man, together with the interests of the true religion, demand that every missionary should sedulously avoid all rudeness, insult or interruption during the observance of the said superstitions; recommending no methods but those adopted by Christ and his apostles, namely, the persevering use of Scripture, reason, prayer, meekness and love.

O that the Lord, who is unconfined by place or condition, may copiously pour out upon you all the rich effusions of his Holy Spirit on the approaching day! My most hearty love to each missionary and each companion, or intended companion of a missionary, who may then encircle the throne of grace. Happy men! Happy women! You are going to be fellow labourers with Christ himself! I congratulate—I almost envy you; yet I love you and can scarcely now forbear dropping a tear of love as each of your names passes across my mind. O what promises are yours and what a reward! Surely heaven is filled with double joy and resounds with unusual acclamations at the arrival of each missionary there. O be faithful, my dear brethren, my dear sisters, be faithful unto death and all this joy is yours! Long as I live, my imagination will be hovering over you in Bengal; and should I die, if separate spirits are allowed a visit to the world they have left, methinks mine would be soon at Mudnabatty, watching your labours, your conflict, and your pleasures, whilst you are always abounding in the work of the Lord.

My dear brother Fuller, pardon me. My feelings have hurried me wither I did not intend. Do not be long without letting me know the progress of affairs. Thanks for your last information. What good news, what encouragement! Pray present my most sincere affection to dear brother Ward in particular, and tell him that I would fain write him a long and loving letter; but I know if he were apprized of the injury it does me at this time, he himself would rather that I omitted it.

Ever yours
S.P.

# 34

# To the Church in Cannon Street, Birmingham[1]

*Plymouth, May 31, 1799*

To the dear people of my charge, the flock of Christ, assembling in Cannon Street, Birmingham, their afflicted but affectionate pastor, presents his love in Christ Jesus, the "great Shepherd of the sheep."[2]

My dearest, dearest friends and brethren,

Separated as I have been a long time from you, and during that time of separation having suffered much both in body and mind, yet my heart has still been with you, participating in your sorrows, uniting in your prayers, and rejoicing with you in the hope of that glory to which divine faithfulness has engaged to bring us and for which our heavenly Father, by all his providences and by every operation of his Holy Spirit, is daily preparing us.

---

1  From Fuller, *Memoirs of the Rev. Samuel Pearce*, 152–156.
2  Hebrews 13:20.

Never, my dear brethren, did I so much rejoice in our being made "partakers of the heavenly calling"[3] as during my late afflictions. The sweet thoughts of glory, where I shall meet my dear Lord Jesus with all his redeemed ones, perfectly freed from all that sin which now burdens us and makes us groan from day to day—this transports my soul, whilst out of weakness I am made strong and at times am enabled to glory even in my bodily infirmities that the power of Christ, in supporting when flesh and heart fail, may the more evidently rest upon me.[4] O my dear brethren and sisters, let me, as one alive almost from the dead, let me exhort you to stand fast in that blessed gospel which for ten years I have now preached among you: the gospel of the grace of God; the gospel of free, full, everlasting salvation, founded on the sufferings and death of "God manifest in the flesh."[5] Look much at this all-amazing scene!... And then say whether any poor broken-hearted sinner need be afraid to venture his hopes of salvation on such a sacrifice, especially since he who is thus mighty to save hath said that "whosoever cometh to him he will in no wise cast out."[6] You, beloved, who have found the peace-speaking virtue of this blood of atonement, must not be satisfied with what you have already known or enjoyed. The only way to be constantly happy and constantly prepared for the most awful changes which we must all experience is to be constantly looking and coming to a dying Saviour; renouncing all our own worthiness; cleaving to the loving Jesus as our all in all; giving up everything, however valuable to our worldly interests, and clashes with our fidelity to Christ; begging that of his fulness we may receive "grace upon grace,"[7] whilst our faith actually relies on his power and faithfulness for the full accomplishment of every promise in his Word that we plead with him; and guarding against everything that might for a moment bring

---

3 Hebrews 3:1.
4 See 2 Corinthians 12:9.
5 1 Timothy 3:16.
6 John 6:37.
7 John 1:16.

distance and darkness between your souls and your precious Lord. If you thus live (and oh that you may daily receive fresh life from Christ so to do!) "the peace of God will keep your hearts and minds"[8] and you will be filled with "joy unspeakable and full of glory."[9]

As a church, you cannot conceive what pleasure I have enjoyed in hearing that you are in peace, that you attend prayer meetings, that you seem to be stirred up of late for the honour and prosperity of religion. Go on in these good ways, my beloved friends, and assuredly "the God of peace will be with you."[10] Yes, if after all I should be taken entirely from you, yet God will surely visit you and never leave you, nor forsake you.

As to my health, I seem on the whole to be still mending, though but very slowly. The fever troubles me often, both by day and night, but my strength increases. I long to see your faces in the flesh; yea, when I thought myself near the gates of the grave, I wished, if it were the Lord's will, to depart among those whom I so much loved. But I am in good hands and all must be right.

I thank both you and the congregation most affectionately for all the kindness you have shown respecting me and my family during my absence. The Lord return it a thousandfold! My love to everyone, both old and young, rich and poor, as though named. The Lord bless to your edification the occasional ministry which you enjoy. I hope you regularly attend upon it and keep together as "the horses in Pharaoh's chariot."[11] I pray much for you; pray, still pray, for your very affectionate, though unworthy, pastor.

P.S. [to Thomas King] I have made an effort to write this letter. My affections would take no denial, but it has brought on the fever.[12]

---

8  Philippians 4:7.
9  1 Peter 1:8.
10  Philippians 4:9.
11  Song of Songs 1:9.
12  Thomas King was one of the deacons of the Cannon Street congregation. See pages 121–122, note 2.

*John Ryland, Jr. (1753–1825)*

# 35

# To John Ryland, Jr.[1]

*Birmingham, July 20, 1799*

My very dear brother,

...I find myself getting weaker and weaker, and so my Lord instructs me in his pleasure to remove me soon. You say well, my dear brother, that at such a prospect, I "cannot complain." No, blessed be his dear name, who shed his blood for me, he helps me to rejoice, at times, with "joy unspeakable."[2] Now I see the value of the religion of the cross. It is a religion for a dying sinner. It is all the most guilty, the most wretched can desire. Yes, I taste its sweetness, and enjoy its fulness, with all the gloom of a dying bed before me. And far rather would I be the poor emaciated and emaciating creature that I am, than be an emperor, with every earthly good about him—but without a God!

I was delighted the other day, in re-perusing the *Pilgrim's Progress*,[3] to observe that when Christian came to the top of the hill Difficulty,

---

1  From Fuller, *Memoirs of the Rev. Samuel Pearce*, 176–178.
2  1 Peter 1:8.
3  This is the famous Christian classic by John Bunyan (1628–1688).

he was put to sleep in a chamber called Peace. "Why how good is the Lord of the way to me!" said I. I have not reached the summit of the hill yet, but notwithstanding he puts me to sleep in the chamber of Peace every night.... True, it is often a chamber of pain; but let pain be as formidable as it may, it has never yet been able to expel that peace, which the great Guardian of Israel has appointed to keep my heart and mind through Christ Jesus.[4]

I have been labouring lately to exercise most love to God when I have been suffering most fervently. But, what shall I say? Alas, too often the sense of pain absorbs every other thought. Yet there have been seasons when I have been affected with such a delightful sense of the loveliness of God as to ravish my soul and give predominance to the sacred passion. It was never till to-day that I got any personal instruction from our Lord's telling Peter by what death he should glorify God.[5] O what a satisfying thought is it, that God appoints those means of dissolution whereby he gets most glory to himself. It was the very thing I needed, for of all the ways of dying, that which I most dreaded was by a consumption; (in which it is now highly probably my disorder will issue.) But, O my dear Lord, if by this death I can most glorify thee, I prefer it to all other, and thank thee that by this mean thou art hastening my fuller enjoyment of thee in a purer world.

A sinless state! "O 'tis a heaven worth dying for!" I cannot realize anything about heaven, but the presence of Christ and his people, and a perfect deliverance from sin, and I want no more. I am sick of sinning. Soon I shall be beyond its power. "O joyful hour! O blest bode! I shall be near and like my God!"

I only thought of filling one side[6]—and now have not left room to thank you and dear Mrs. Ryland for the minute, affectionate and

---

4  See Philippians 4:7.
5  See John 21:18–19.
6  That is, one side of the letter.

constant attentions you paid us in Bristol. May the Lord reward you. Our hearty love to all around, till we meet in heaven.

Eternally yours in Christ,

S.P.

# Selected letters of
# Sarah Pearce

After the death of her husband, Sarah Pearce noted that she had been "deeply interested in all that interested" her Samuel.[1] Given this, it is not at all inappropriate to include some of her letters in this volume. Widowhood was a very difficult time for Sarah, for she keenly missed her husband, who had been her best earthly friend. The extracts from her letters that follow reveal the sterling nature of her Christianity.[2] Her faith has a very human face as she wrestles with grief and widowhood, but it is also one that is imbued with the joy of knowing Christ and the hope of spending eternity with him. She also was called upon to bury one of their five children between her husband's death and her own on May 25, 1804.

---

1   Letter to William Rogers, June 16, 1801, in "Original Letters, of the Rev. Samuel Pearce," *The Religious Remembrancer* (October 1, 1814): 19.

2   Apart from one letter, all of these extracts come from [Andrew Fuller?], "Memoir of Mrs. Pearce," *The Theological and Biblical Magazine*, 5 (1805): 1–8, *passim*. The only changes that have been made to the text of these letters is some minor editorial changes in punctuation. This edited version of these extracts from Sarah Pearce's letters first appeared in Michael A.G. Haykin, ed., "'As Gold Refined':The Piety of Sarah Hopkins Pearce," *The Gospel Witness*, 83, No.4 (September 2004): 11–12. Used by permission.

Unlike Samuel, of whom a number of portraits exist, there is none of Sarah—unless it be the one sketched by her words and those of her beloved Samuel to her and about her. A rare article by Joseph Belcher about her, "The Wife of Samuel Pearce," is a helpful study, though written in typical florid Victorian prose. Belcher is best known for his three-volume edition of the works of Pearce's biographer, Andrew Fuller. He had actually grown up in Pearce's Cannon Street congregation where he was converted in 1814. When Belcher's mother was dying in 1800, Sarah Pearce took the time to visit the dying woman. It was but a few weeks after Samuel had died, but Sarah sought to put aside her own grief and alleviate the sufferings of others. Joseph never forgot that visit from Sarah and her two children Anna and William, and the way that, after conversing with his mother, Sarah took Joseph and his sister apart to another room where she prayed for their ultimate happiness. Belcher had no doubt God eventually heard those prayers.[3] Belcher remembered Sarah as a woman of remarkable piety with a winsome personality though somewhat shy. In regard to the latter trait he likened her to "the lonely lily of the valley" that diffuses its fragrance though unseen.[4]

---

3  "The Wife of Samuel Pearce," *The Mothers Journal and Family Visitant*, 19 (1854): 11.

4  "The Wife of Samuel Pearce," 11–12.

# 36

## To Mrs. Harwood[1]

### December 25, 1799

In vain, alas, in vain I seek him whose presence gave a zest to every enjoyment! I wander about the house as one bereft of her better half. I go into the study—I say to myself, "There is the chair he occupied, there are the books he read; but where, oh where is the owner?" I come into the parlour—there my tenderest feelings are awakened by four fatherless children.[2] The loss of him with whom I have been accustomed to go up to the house of God diminishes, ah, I may say too frequently deprives me of, my enjoyment while there.

---

1 This letter was written but eleven weeks after her husband's death. According to the "Memoir of Mrs. Pearce," 2, n.*, Mrs. Harwood lived in Bristol. She was probably related to John Harwood, a Cannon Street deacon. On John Harwood, see "Some Samuel Pearce Documents," *The Baptist Quarterly* 18 (1959–1960): 29–30.

2 Her eldest son, William Hopkins Pearce (1794–1840), was away from home, having gone to live with Pastor William Nichols (1762–1835) of Collingham, near Nottingham. William eventually went to India as a missionary. See the *Memoirs of the Rev. W.H. Pearce* (Calcutta: Baptist Mission Press, 1841). Regretfully, his main recollection of his father was the time of the funeral and seeing his father's coffin (*Memoirs of the Rev. W.H. Pearce*, 2).

# 37

## *To Mrs. Franklin*[1]

*Alcester, July 11, 1800*

After an illness of a few days, it hath pleased the great Arbiter of life and death to bereave me of my dear little boy, aged one year and six months, and thus again to convince me of the uncertainty of all earthly joys and bring to remembrance my past sorrows. He was in my fond eyes one of the fairest flowers human nature ever exhibited; but ah, he is dropt at an early period! Yet the hope of his being transplanted into a more salutary clime, there to re-bloom in everlasting vigour, and the reflection that if he had lived, he had unavoidably been exposed to innumerable temptations,

---

1   This was written not long after the Pearce's youngest child, Samuel, died. Mrs. Franklin lived in Coventry. See "Memoir of Mrs. Pearce," 2, n.*. Mrs. Franklin was the wife of Francis Franklin (c.1773–1852), a Bristol alumnus and pastor of the Cow Lane Baptist Chapel, Coventry, from 1798 to 1852. Their daughters, the Misses Franklin—Mary and Rebecca—presided over a school that the novelist George Eliot (1819–1880) attended. Apparently Eliot based the character of Rufus Lyon in her novel *Felix Holt, the Radical* (1866) on Francis Franklin. See A.C. Underwood, *A History of the English Baptists* (London: Carey Kingsgate Press Ltd., 1956), 175, n.1. For the identification of "Mrs. Franklin," see Belcher, "Wife of Samuel Pearce," 40.

from which if my life was spared, I should yet be unable to screen him, make me still. Though I feel as a parent and I hope as a Christian, yet I can resign him.[2]

Oh could I feel but half the resignation respecting the loss of my beloved Pearce! But I cannot. Still bleeds the deep, deep wound; and a return to Birmingham[3] is a return to the most poignant feelings. I wish however to resign him to the hand that gave and that had an unquestionable right to take away. Be still then every tumultuous passion, and know that he who hath inflicted these repeated strokes is God: that God whom I desire to reverence under every painful dispensation, being persuaded that what I know not now, I shall know hereafter.

---

2  Thomas Morgan (1776–1857), Pearce's successor as pastor of Cannon Street Baptist Church, conducted the funeral of young Samuel.

3  This letter was written from Alcester, which is not far from Birmingham.

# 38

## To Mrs. Franklin

*December 1800*

Since I saw you, my heart has been rent with such passions as are indescribable and which I shudder to reflect upon. But let me speak it with unfeigned gratitude. I have felt for this last week a degree of resignation, to which, ever since I lost my beloved Pearce, I was a stranger. From comparing my own insignificance with the greatness of the hand that has visited me, and who though he smote me (as I fear) in wrath, yet hath remembered mercy, my spirit has bowed to his sovereign will. I have also felt that it is of the Lord's mercies I am not consumed. I had said by my thoughts and actions, "Let all go: there is nothing worth keeping!" Why then was I not deprived of every comfort, seeing I made so light of what was left? To what a state should I have been reduced had the Lord taken me at my word! But oh, cheering thought! He is a God full of compassion who does not afflict willingly; and I believe I shall see in the end that all that hath befallen me is for my profit.

*William Rogers (1751–1824)*

# 39

## *To William Rogers*[1]

*Birmingham, England, June 16, 1801*

Reverend and dear sir,

My good friend Mr. Potts put into my hand your very kind and affectionate letter addressed to him, and requested I would write you. A persuasion that you look more at the state of the writer's heart, than the precision of the pen, encourages me to attempt to comply with his request: the kind regard in his letter, expressed for my much beloved and ever-to-be regretted partner, was very grateful to my heart, and demands some exertion on my part, and were my abilities adequate to my wishes, I would not be behind you in a grateful return. But the depression of mind under which I have more or less constantly laboured for a long period has almost incapacitated me from epistolary converse; this apology, and a natural disinclination for writing, will, I hope my dear sir, be admitted by you for suffering you to remain so long ignorant respecting the safety of your very affectionate and valuable letter, dated July 10,

---

1 From *The Religious Remembrancer* (October 1, 1814): 19.

1799, which I received by a friend of the Rev. Mr. Medley,[2] (for he alas! is no more) and came too late for my dear Mr. Pearce to read or hear it read to him, as it arrived but three days before he bade adieu to all mortal friendships; had he been able to have read it, I am well assured it would have afforded him sincere pleasure and have been acknowledged with gratitude. Please to accept all that he would have said, from one deeply interested in all that interested him.

...Had you known my dear Mr. Pearce, and witnessed the happiness I enjoyed from him in the nearest of all earthly connexions, you would not wonder when I say I needed all the consolations of that Friend who was born for adversity,[3] when this connexion was dissolved, to support the heavy stroke; and you must rejoice with me when I tell you he was not totally absent, for though he has visited me with stroke upon stroke, I trust he has not forgotten to be gracious, or in anger shut up his tender mercies. I hope never to lose sight of the goodness of God under the sharpest trials. He has an indisputable right to do with me and mine as seemeth him good. It is the consideration of the justice, wisdom, power and goodness of God, united with every perfection of Deity that has calmed and supported me through all. Nature has felt, and that most poignantly—my health has suffered, and my mind has participated [in] the weakness of my mortal frame, and for some time my thoughts could scarcely rise beyond the gloomy grave. The dear objects of my tenderest regret claimed all, and had it not been for the idea of rejoining them to part no more, but to be forever with

---

2  Samuel Medley (1738–1799) was the Pastor of Byrom Street Baptist Church, Liverpool. For a study of his life and ministry, see B.A. Ramsbottom, *Samuel Medley: Preacher, Pastor, Poet* (n.p.: The Fauconberg Press for The Strict Baptist Historical Society, 1978).

3  Sarah is recalling Proverbs 17:17, which actually runs thus in the King James Version: "A friend loveth at all times, and a brother is born for adversity."

the Lord,[4] my heart would long ago have sunk under these repeated strokes; for since he deprived me of my invaluable partner, he has also taken from me a dear little babe who bore the name of its father, and, in my fond eyes, one of the fairest and most lovely blossoms human nature ever displayed—though alas! withered and dropped at an early period.

Well, my dear sir, the time is hastening when all these mysterious providences shall be explained to the satisfaction of all who love and serve the Lord our God in sincerity and truth. Happy, glorious day! Oh may I be amongst them there, and love, adore and praise. I have still left two dear little boys and [a] girl, and I sometimes hope they will prove a comfort to me; but ah, how uncertain is distant good—will you pray for them, my dear sir, that they may tread in the steps of their dear departed father, and that I may realize that happiness in them which I have enjoyed in a near connexion, in a higher degree than most—and oh! pray that the trials I have been exercised with may be sanctified for my increase in faith, patience, and conformity to God. For though my happiness as to this world is bounded, I have much to be thankful for; God is good, and has not left me without a hope that cheers the gloom of life and points to brighter worlds.

…Permit me to share in the joy occasioned by your's to Mr. Potts, by the news of the prosperity of Zion in the United States; what news so animating to a serious mind. May this be but the drop before a copious shower, till our dear Lord shall have the uttermost parts of the earth for his possession.

I will detain you no longer, my dear sir, than while subscribing myself your's most respectfully,

Sarah Pearce.

---

4  Cf. 1 Thessalonians 4:17.

# 40

## To Mrs. Harwood

September 19, 1801

It is an unspeakable mercy that I am in the hands of so kind and good a God, who "knoweth our frame and remembereth that we are but dust."[1] "As a father pitieth his children, so the Lord pitieth them that fear him."[2] How light and trifling do all our trials appear when compared with the important end they are designed to answer. What are the sufferings of the present time "compared with the glory that is to be revealed in us"?[3] May we be made willing to do and suffer the whole of God's will, in order to our meetness for the inheritance of the saints in light! O that my heart were more in heaven, where I trust my treasure is! At times I can say, "Do with me, Lord, as seemeth thee good; only sanctify thy dealings with me, and bring me forth as gold refined from all remaining dross."

---

1  Psalm 103:14.
2  Psalm 103:13.
3  Romans 8:18.

# 41

## To Mrs. Franklin

*October 12, 1801*

No doubt you have joined the general joy occasioned by the sound of peace.[1] Never did I experience such sensations as on last Saturday and last Sabbath Day. You may perhaps recollect that Saturday, October 10, is an ever memorable day to me![2] I do not know that ever I spent a day more devoted to sadness. My situation is retired—no friend came near me—every painful feeling was again recalled—I indulged it; my whole heart took its fill of grief! You may suppose I was ill prepared for attending the service of the sanctuary next day; and for a while I felt a desire of staying at home, but did not think it right to indulge it. At length I summoned resolution and went. While on the road, peace! peace! was sounded in my ears; every eye beamed gladness; but my poor harp was hung

---

1 This is a reference to peace negotiations in 1801 between the British government and that of Napoleon Bonaparte (1769–1821) in France that sought to end the world war that had raged between the British and the French from 1793 to that point in time.

2 Samuel Pearce died on this day in 1799.

upon the willows. Oh how I wished to hide myself in a corner where no eye could see me. I was, however, considerably relieved in the morning from a sermon by Mr. Giles of Dartmouth, on "Our light affliction, which is but for a moment, working for us a far more exceeding and eternal weight of glory."[3] My burden was in some measure removed.

---

3  2 Corinthians 4:17. William Giles (1771–1846) was the minister of the Baptist Church in Dartmouth, Devonshire. He had been a Methodist missionary to Sierra Leone for about six months in 1796, and, on the voyage home, study of the Scriptures led him to Baptist convictions. He was baptized subsequently by Isaiah Birt. According to one of his daughters, Mary Eliza Godfrey (1795–1884), his ministry at Dartmouth, from 1797 to 1809, was attended with "great persecution for the Gospel's sake" (http://www.dartmouth-history.org.uk/content_images/upload/My_Dear_Children.htm; accessed July 1, 2011). Giles' son, also William Giles (1798–1856) and a Baptist minister, was the first schoolmaster of the famous Victorian novelist, Charles Dickens (1812–1870). For some of these details, I am indebted to Chris Pigott, "Reverend John Eustace Giles, Baptist Minister," July 2, 2008 entry of *The Pigott Family of Queen's County, Ireland; Some Ancestral Connections* (http://pigott-gorrie.blogspot.com/2008/07/reverend-john-eustace-giles-baptist.html; accessed July 2, 2011).

# 42

## To Mrs. Franklin[1]

I am just returned from hearing two more of our friends declare before the church what God hath done for their souls; and my dear Pearce was the instrument of bringing them out of darkness into marvellous light. Rejoice with me that the seed so long sown springs up. Gratitude excites a desire to praise my God, the gracious Giver of every mercy.

Oh, my friend, how rich, how inestimable is the gift of Jesus Christ! All that eye hath seen, or the most lively imagination conceived of, is nothing to the extent of the divine goodness. Never shall we form any adequate conception of it till we know as we are known. To be near and like God, must surely be the summit of expected felicity. Oh delightful thought! It will never decay. May a lively and increasing hope in these exalted realities, enable us to bear every trial with patience and fortitude. He who is a rock, and whose work is perfect, will accomplish whatever concerns those who put their trust in him. I could not withhold news which has caused such a gleam of joy as I have not experiences for a long time, from my dear friend, who has taken so large a share of my gloom. Farewell.

---

1 This letter is undated.

# Lines written on the words of Ignatius of Antioch, "My love is crucified"

*January 19, 1795*

Warm was his heart, his faith was strong,
  Who thus in rapture cried
When on his way to martyrdom,
  My love is crucified.

Warm also be my love for him,
  Who thus for sinners died;
Long as I live be this my theme,
  My love is crucified....

When first my soul by living faith,
  My bleeding Lord espied,
My lips declar'd at every breath,
  My love is crucified.

And since my happy heart has known
  His sacred blood applied,
This still has been my sweetest song,
  My love is crucified.

—*Samuel Pearce*

# Annotated bibliography

The earliest account of Pearce's life and ministry is Andrew Fuller's *Memoirs of the Rev. Samuel Pearce. A.M.*, which was written out of Fuller's deep affection for Pearce and the conviction that he and his friends had known a truly remarkable Christian. Before Pearce died, Fuller told him that he fully intended to write something about him. As he told Pearce:

> ...you need not fear that I will puff off your character, any more than you would mine. We are all of us, God knows it, poor unworthy creatures. Yet the truth may be told to the glory of sovereign grace; and I long to express my inextinguishable affection for you in something more than words, I mean by doing something that shall be of use to your family.[1]

The final sentence of this quote refers to the fact that the monies

---

1  Letter to Samuel Pearce, August 30, 1799, in Ernest A. Payne, "Some Sidelights on Pearce and His Friends," *The Baptist Quarterly*, 7 (1934–1935): 275.

from the sale of the book were to be given to Sarah. First published in 1800, Fuller's memoir of his friend went through four editions by 1816, the year following Fuller's death. During the nineteenth century, it was reprinted in various editions on both sides of the Atlantic and acquired the status of a minor spiritual classic. It is available today as *A Heart for Missions: The Classic Memoir of Samuel Pearce* (Birmingham, Alabama: Solid Ground Christian Books, 2006).

Not until the early twentieth century did another significant biography of Pearce appear. This was by Pearce's great-grandson, S. Pearce Carey (1862–1953), who is best known for his massive biography of his other great-grandfather, William Carey. His *Samuel Pearce, M.A., The Baptist Brainerd* (London: Carey Press, 1913) went through three editions: two in 1913 (in April and August[2]) and a third and final undated edition, which was probably published in 1922.[3] It turned out to be the only book-length biography of Pearce in the twentieth century. When S. Pearce Carey wrote this biography he was not aware of the love letters of Pearce to his wife. When these came to light in the 1930s, he wrote a small piece, "Love Letters of Samuel Pearce," *The Baptist Quarterly*, 8 (1936–1937): 96–102.

One of the most prolific twentieth-century students of the English Calvinistic Baptist community was Ernest A. Payne, who also wrote a number of noteworthy studies of Pearce: "Some Sidelights on Pearce and His Friends," *The Baptist Quarterly*, 7 (1934–1935): 270–275; *The First Generation: Early Leaders of the Baptist Missionary Society in England and America* (London: Carey Press,

---

2 See the "Preface to the Second Edition," which is dated August 1913 and mentions that the first edition appeared at "the end of April" [*Samuel Pearce, M.A., The Baptist Brainerd* (London: Carey Press, 1913), 11]. I am grateful to Rev. Gary Long, of Springfield, Missouri, for access to this second edition.

3 In the dedication to the third edition, S. Pearce Carey mentions the fact that his older brother, William Carey, had served in India for thirty-seven years. He had gone out to India in 1885.

1936), 46–54; and "Some Samuel Pearce Documents," *The Baptist Quarterly*, 18 (1959–1960): 26–34.

Neither S. Pearce Carey nor Ernest Payne would have identified themselves with the evangelical Calvinism in which Pearce delighted. In the past sixty years, however, there has been a tremendous recovery of this Calvinism, and with it has come renewed appreciation for Pearce, as is evident in the following studies: Paul Helm, "Samuel Pearce," *Free Grace Record*, 2, No.9 (Winter 1962): 273–279; Faith Cook, "Samuel Pearce" in her *Sound of Trumpets* (Edinburgh/Carlisle, Pennsylvania: The Banner of Truth Trust, 1999), 145–176; Tom Wells, "Samuel Pearce (1766–1799)" in Michael A.G. Haykin, ed., *British Particular Baptists, 1638–1910* (Springfield, Missouri: Particular Baptist Press, 2000), II, 182–199; Robert Oliver, "The Seraphic Samuel Pearce" in *Puritans and Spiritual Life. Papers Read at the 2001 Westminster Conference* (London: The Westminster Conference, 2001), 103–118. With this renewed embrace of the theology of Pearce and his friends, the time is right for a new biography of "the seraphic Pearce."

# Reading spiritual classics

*by Michael A.G. Haykin, series editor*

In recent days, "spirituality" has become something of a buzzword in Reformed circles. This is all well and good. But there is a downside to the story. The spiritual books being read are often drawn from streams that are seriously deficient when it comes to the truths in which Reformed believers delight. This series has been designed to partially fill the gap by providing choice selections from various Reformed writers.

The reading of spiritual classics should differ from other types of reading. Whereas one reads a newspaper, dictionary or textbook for factual information or immediate answers to queries, in spiritual reading one seeks to inflame the heart as well as to inform the mind. Spiritual reading, as Eugene Peterson has noted, should therefore be "leisurely, repetitive, reflective reading." It should not be hurried, for attention needs to be paid to what the Spirit of God is saying through the text. And texts rich in spiritual nourishment beg to be read again and again so that their truth and beauty might be savoured.

Of course, when it comes to spiritual classics, the Bible occupies a unique and indispensable place. It is the fountainhead and source of the Christian faith. Anyone wishing to make progress as a disciple of Christ must be committed to regular reflection and meditation on the Scriptures. Blessed is the believer whose delight is in the Word of God, on which he or she "meditates day and night" (Psalm 1:1–2).

But we are neither the first to read the Scriptures nor the first to meditate extensively on them. Christians of previous days also found strength and nourishment by meditating on the Word of God. Often their wisdom and insight was recorded—either in books, diaries, letters, hymns or sermons—and these, having been preserved, we are in the habit of calling spiritual classics. Such classics have a way of sending their readers back to the Bible with deeper insight into the nature of the Christian faith and cultivate a greater desire to seek after Christ's glory and blessed presence.

Other titles available from Joshua Press...

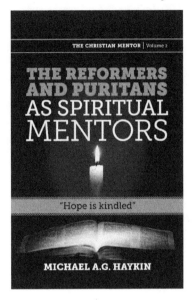

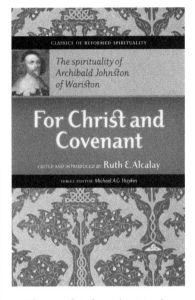

*The Christian Mentor* | *Volume 2*

# The Reformers and Puritans as spiritual mentors
"Hope is kindled"
*By Michael A. G. Haykin*

REFORMERS SUCH as Tyndale, Cranmer and Calvin, and Puritans Richard Greenham, John Owen, etc. are examined to see how their display of the light of the gospel provides us with models of Christian conviction and living who can speak into our lives today.

ISBN 978–1-894400–39–8

*Classics of Reformed spirituality*

# For Christ and Covenant
The spirituality of Archibald Johnston of Wariston
*By Ruth E. Alcalay*

ARCHIBALD JOHNSTON WAS one of mid-seventeenth-century Scotland's most influential religious and political figures. Through excerpts from his diary and speeches, we are given a window into his relationship with God.

ISBN 978-1-894400-36–7

*Other titles available from Joshua Press...*

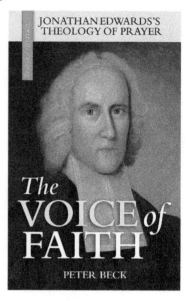

| Great themes in Puritan preaching | The voice of faith |
|---|---|
| *Compiled and edited By Mariano Di Gangi* | *Jonathan Edwards's theology of prayer*<br>*By Peter Beck* |

## Great themes in Puritan preaching

*Compiled and edited*
*By Mariano Di Gangi*

DRAWING FROM a gold mine of Puritan writings, this book provides a taste of the riches of Puritan theology and its application to life. This title will whet your appetite and stir your faith to greater views of Christ, his Person and his work.

ISBN 978–1-894400-26–8 (HC)

ISBN 978–1-894400-24–4 (PB)

## The voice of faith
### Jonathan Edwards's theology of prayer
*By Peter Beck*

EXPLORING THE sermons and writings of Jonathan Edwards, Dr. Beck draws a comprehensive picture of his theology of prayer and why Edwards believed God would hear the prayers of his people. Interspersed are three external biographies that set the historical and theological scene.

ISBN 978–1-894400-33–6 (HC)

ISBN 978–1-894400-32–9 (PB)

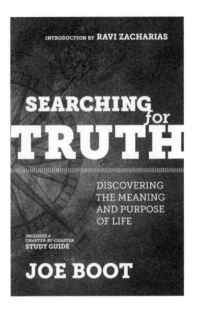

# Friendship

*By Hugh Black*

HUGH BLACK addresses the challenges and responsibilities of friendship, including the consequences of wrecked friendships. In true friendship, accountability and love inspire us to live with more honour, integrity and grace. Ultimately, we see that in Jesus Christ we can have that "higher friendship," which revolutionizes the way we live and think, and what we value.

ISBN 978-1-894400-28-2 (HC)
ISBN 978-1-894400-27-5 (PB)

# Searching for truth

*Discovering the meaning and purpose of life*
*By Joe Boot*

BEGINNING WITH a basic understanding of the world, Joe Boot explains the biblical worldview, giving special attention to the life and claims of Jesus Christ. He wrestles with questions about suffering, truth, morality and guilt.

ISBN 978-1-894400-40-4